Fountain Series in Law and Business Studies

Criminal Law in Uganda

Sexual Assaults and Offences Against Morality

Lillian Tibatemwa-Ekirikubinza

FOUNTAIN PUBLISHERS
Kampala

Fountain Publishers Ltd
P.O. Box 488
Kampala, Uganda
Email: fountain@starcom.co.ug
Website: www.fountainpublishers.co.ug

Distributed in Europe, North America and Australia by African Books Collective Ltd (ABC), Unit 13, Kings Meadow, Ferry Hinksey Road, Oxford OX2 0DP, United Kingdom.
Tel: 44(0) 1865-726686, Fax:44(0)1865-793298.
E-mail: abc@africanbookscollective.com
Website: www.africanbookscollective.com

ISBN 9970-02-478-7

Acknowlegements

I am grateful to the Faculty of Law, Makerere University for the funds which enabled me to carry out the research for this book. My gratitude also goes to my two Research Assistants — Stephen Kagoda and Ronald Kalungi — who tirelessly searched through piles of dusty records in order to avail me with cases for analysis.

Cataloguing-in-Publishing Data

Tibatemwa-Ekirikubinza, Lillian
Criminal law in Uganda: sexual assaults and offences against morality.– Kampala: Fountain Publishers, 2005
__ p. __ cm

ISBN 9970 02 478 7

1. Criminal Law – Uganda   2. Sexual Assaults and Offences Against Morality – Uganda
I. Lillian Tibatemwa-Ekirikubinza.   II. Title

Dedication

To Caroline and Christopher Tibatemwa
Thank you for valuing me as a girl child

Contents

List of Abbreviations

Law Reports
AC: Appeals Cases
All ER: All England Reports
CLR: Commonwealth Law Reports
Cox CC: Cox's Criminal Law Cases
Crim App Rep: Criminal Appeal Reports
Crim LR: Criminal Law Revision
EA: East African Law Reports
EACA: East African Court of Appeal Cases
EALR: East African Law Reports
ER: England Reports
HCB: High Court Bulletin
HCCSC: High Court Criminal Session Case
KALR: Kampala Law Report
KB: King's Bench
QB: Queen's Bench
QBD: Queens Bench Division
SLT: Scots Law Times
ULR: Uganda Law Reports
WLR: Weekly Law Reports

Preface

This text book is the second volume in a series of publications on Criminal Law in Uganda. The first volume is entitled *Homicides and Non-Fatal Assaults*. As was the case in *Homicides and Non-Fatal Assaults*, this present work is a presentation on the substantive law on crime in Uganda. It is based on judicial interpretation of the Uganda Penal Code Act – the principal criminal legislation of the country. Although the purpose of the book is a discussion of the major sexual offences created by the Penal Code Act, I have included expositions on some rules of evidence in so far as it is necessary for an understanding of the relevant substantive criminal law.

In 1930 Britain introduced a Model Criminal Code in several of its colonies, including Uganda. Although the Uganda Penal Code in its present form is still principally a reflection of criminal law as it existed in Britain in 1930, over the years the Uganda Judiciary has interpreted principles of criminal law based on our society's political, cultural, social and economic circumstances, and thereby developed its own jurisprudence. In some cases this has led to fundamental departures from English judge-made law. It is thus necessary to record the law as interpreted and understood within the Ugandan context. Consequently, the book is a result of a perusal of records of the High Court of Uganda, the Court of Appeal and the Uganda Supreme Court. Focus was limited to decisions at these three levels of the judiciary because it is these courts which are courts of record. This means that their decisions are binding on lower courts.

It is however noted that up to the early 1970s, Uganda, Kenya and Tanzania shared the services of a joint appellate court: the Court of Appeal for Eastern Africa. Although the court was only an appellate court from the decisions of the national High Courts of each country, its decisions as the highest court in all the three countries were binding on all the three jurisdictions. The reader will thus notice extensive use of judgements by the East African Court of Appeal.

At the time of independence for Uganda, Kenya, Tanganyika, Malawi and Zambia the criminal codes of these countries were almost identical. They were all a result of the Model Criminal Code introduced into each of these countries in 1930 by the British colonial 'masters'. Each of these countries has over the years made changes to its law. Some changes have been in the form of the creation of new offences whereas some have constituted amendments to already existing offences. Nevertheless one can confidently say that the penal codes are still in *pari materia*. It is however unfortunate that in each of these countries there is hardly any book authored on substantive criminal law based on the statutory provisions as interpreted by the national courts of the independent states. It is for this reason that this book will offer invaluable reading not only to students and scholars of the law of crime in Uganda but also to students in the other sister countries.

Teachers of criminal law in each of these countries still refer students to criminal law books based on English law such as Card, Cross and Jones; Smith and Hogan – both titles *Criminal Law*. Books coming out of England today are based on the current English law. Yet England has consistently come up with new statutes on different aspects of criminal law and consequently the current English law is often very different from the 'English' law introduced into colonial Africa in 1930. And as already mentioned the independent states, too, have come up with new statutes which represent a departure from English law, not just as introduced in 1930 but different from the current English law. These developments (in England and in the independent states) make books coming out of England today more and more irrelevant to the jurisprudence of South-Eastern Africa. This book is designed to fill that gap.

In presenting what the law is, I am keenly aware that whereas it may be obvious that offences such as murder, theft and assaults are injurious to individuals as well as to society as a whole, and are thus deserving of being criminalised, there may be disagreements on whether 'victimless' crimes such as incest between adults, prostitution, homosexuality, etc. should be punished by the criminal law. Where possible I have (albeit briefly) presented the views of groups which support criminalisation on the one hand, and those which support decriminalisation of the relevant conduct on the other hand.

I further note that there is need to analyse criminal law in the light of the wider policy issues of contemporary society. This will help students and scholars to appreciate the law within the Uganda specific context. In discussing some of the offences therefore I have *inter alia* made reference to the significance of issues such as:

1. Gender and Women's Human Rights
2. Children's Rights
3. Human Rights
4. Constitutionalism

The book is therefore not just a presentation of substantive law, but in addition it answers questions of how wider policy issues have impacted or should impact on criminal law. Hopefully, students will come out better prepared to deal with issues of law reform, especially from a human rights perspective.

The reader will note that in the presentation of each case I indicate the level of court at which the particular decision was made. This is of value in light of the principle of judicial precedent. Each court is bound by the decisions of the court above it. Thus the decision of the High Court binds all magistrates' courts. A decision of the Court of Appeal binds itself and all lower courts, i.e. High Court and magistrates' courts. By tradition individual judges of the High Court are not absolutely bound by the decisions of other high court judges, but in practice they usually follow such decisions. This is because judicial courtesy requires that a judge does not lightly dissent from the considered opinion of another learned judge. Decisions of the Supreme Court bind itself and all the lower courts, i.e. the Court of Appeal, the High Court and all Magistrates' Courts. As long as no higher court has departed from the interpretation of the law by a lower court, the interpretation of that lower court remains the law. This arises out of the doctrine of *stare decisis* which means that the courts abide by former precedents where the same points of law arise again in litigation.

The system of judicial precedent is dependent upon the existence of good law reporting. Each year the courts of record hear thousands of cases, but the state of law reporting in Uganda is unsatisfactory. Consequently, although the main targets of the publication are students and scholars of criminal law, there is no doubt that the book will be invaluable to judicial officers and practising lawyers.

I must also make mention of the fact that direct quotations of sections of the Penal Code Act by the author are according to Chapter 120 Laws of Uganda, Revised Edition 2000. However, references to sections of the law in court judgements are references to sections as they stood before publication of the revised laws and are thus according to the then Chapter 106 of the Laws of Uganda.

Dr Lillian Tibatemwa-Ekirikubinza.
February 2005

Introduction

This book deals with offences referred to by Chapter XIV of the Uganda Penal Code Act[1] as 'Offences against Morality'. My use of the phrase 'sexual assault' in the title is however very deliberate. It is meant to bring out the violence inherent in non-consensual and/or abusive sexual conduct. Although the Penal Code criminalises some instances in which violence is used in order to 'secure' submission to sexual advances, the violent nature of the crime has been sidelined. Instead of the conduct being called what it is – an assault, a violent act – the moral issues involved in sex and sexuality have been placed at the forefront. As a result, offences which constitute violent conduct of a sexual nature[2] have been lumped together with other sexual conduct which may violate 'accepted' sexual norms and values of society but may not infringe the rights of any particular individual. The latter conduct involves no violence and is based on voluntary or consensual sexual relations between the parties.[3] I nevertheless note that both types of conduct (the consensual and the non-consensual) referred to by the Code as 'offences against morality' have one thing in common – they involve sexual conduct. It would seem that in the context of the Penal Code Act, immorality is synonymous with sexual 'misconduct'.

Moralising sexual assaults is erroneous for as aptly put by the Uganda Court of Appeal in *Kayondo Robert v Uganda* Criminal Appeal No. 18/96:

> The essence of the crime of rape is not the fact of intercourse but the injury and outrage to the modesty and feelings of the woman by means of sexual intercourse feloniously and *forcefully* effected. (My emphasis)

Indeed it must be emphasised that sexual assaults are fundamentally acts of violence, not acts of passion. I agree with MacFarlane (2004) who stated that:

> Sexual assault is much more an issue of power, domination, control, invasion, humiliation ... It is about women losing control of their safety, losing autonomy over their bodies, and often fearing for their lives while being subjected to an attack ... And it is the experience of that fear [of death] that creates the significant physical and emotional disturbances in victims (both short term and long term) identified as rape trauma syndrome. (p. 78)

The book also deals with some offences falling under Chapter XV of the Uganda Penal Code entitled 'Offences Relating to Marriage and Domestic Obligations', e.g. adultery, elopement and bigamy. The said offences involve violations of sexual norms and thus share much in common with the other so-called offences against morality, which are not violent in nature. It is for this reason that I discuss them here.

A discussion of the various offences will bring out the criminal law's attempt to regulate sexual behaviour and its support for society's parameters of 'normal' sexual behaviour.

The following offences will be discussed:
- Rape under Sections 123, 124 and 125 of the Uganda Penal Code

- Defilement of girls under the age of 18 years under Section 129 of the Uganda Penal Code
- Defilement of idiots or imbeciles under Section 130 of the Uganda Penal Code
- Indecent assaults of females under Section 128 of the Uganda Penal Code
- Indecent assaults of boys under 18 years of age, under Section 147 of the Uganda Penal Code
- Prostitution and related offences under Sections 136-139 of the Uganda Penal Code
- Unnatural offences under Sections 145 and 146 of the Uganda Penal Code
- Incest under Sections 149-151 of the Uganda Penal Code
- Adultery under Section 154 of the Uganda Penal Code
- Elopement under Section 127 of the Uganda Penal Code

In discussing the various sexual offences it is important to point out the amendments that were made to the Penal Code Act in 1990. The Penal Code (Amendment) Statute of 1990[4] led to the following changes in the law:

- Creation of new offences
- Raised penalties for most sexual offences
- Amendments to already existing offences

In its preamble the purpose of the Statute was said to be:

> ... providing for additional sexual offences punishable by law in order to protect the family as an institution, to safeguard women, children and young persons from sexual abuse, to curb the spread of endemic disease and generally to increase penalties for other related offences ...

The particular changes made will be specifically discussed along with the relevant provisions.

---

1. Chapter 120 Laws of Uganda (Revised Edition 2000).
2. An example is the offence of rape.
3. E.g. prostitution, incest between consenting adults and unnatural offences. For such offences 'it is society that is the victim.'
4. Statute 4A

2

The Law on Rape:
Sections 123-125 of the Uganda Penal Code

Definition of Rape: Section 123 Uganda Penal Code[1]

> Any person who has unlawful carnal knowledge of a woman or girl, without her consent, or with her consent, if the consent is obtained by force or by means of threats or intimidation of any kind, or by fear of bodily harm, or by means of false representation as to the nature of the act, or in the case of a married woman, by personating her husband, is guilty of the felony termed rape.

Simply stated rape occurs when a male person has sexual intercourse with a woman who is not his wife, and the sexual intercourse takes place without the woman's consent.
The ingredients that must be proved by the prosecution are:
- Carnal knowledge
- Of a female
- The carnal knowledge must be unlawful
- Absence of consent

Punishment for rape
Section 124[2] of the Code provides that a person convicted of rape is liable to suffer death. Prior to the 1990 amendment the maximum penalty for rape was life imprisonment. It is however noted that the penalty is not mandatory and thus it is expected that the court will use its discretion to determine the exact punishment in any particular case.
Apart from the rise in sentence the offence of rape was left untouched by the 1990 amendment to the law.

Who can commit rape?
A male person
Under the law of rape it is only a male person who can be guilty as a direct participant in a rape case. This definition is based on the meaning of the phrase 'carnal knowledge' discussed later on in the chapter, that is, penetration of the female organ by the male organ. But although it is only a male person who can be guilty of directly participating in a rape, a female who aids a male person in perpetrating the rape of another female can be guilty of rape under the general rule of principal offenders which covers not only a person who actually does the act which constitutes the offence, but also those who help that person in engaging in the unlawful behaviour.[3]

The law and a male person of under 14 years
A boy under the age of 14 years is presumed incapable of penetrative sex.[4] No evidence is admissible to show that a particular boy under 14 years old is in fact physically capable of the act.[5] But as has been stated in regard to a female person, a boy under

the age of 14 years could be guilty of rape as an aider and abettor.

CASE: *Uganda v Lt Col Issa Habib Galungube* High Court Criminal Session Case No. 30/89

It was stated *inter alia* that the phrase 'Any person' in Section 117 Penal Code Act (now 123) refers to a male person of the age of 14 years and above, since ' ... in law, a person below fourteen years of age cannot commit the offence of rape.'

It has been argued by Angela Davis (1983) that in capitalist societies rape laws were originally framed not to protect women, but rather to protect upper class men whose daughters and wives might be assaulted.[6] The law was primarily interested in protecting the male property in the female body. It was akin to offences such as burglary. MacFarlane (2004) also reports that:

> Development of the law concerning the offence of rape did not get off to a very good start. In earlier times, the offence was linked more with notions of property and theft than with principles concerning the security of the person. (p. 76)

The law was intended to protect man's right to determine the circumstances of procreation.[7] It is for this reason that originally the emission of semen was a necessary ingredient for a conviction. Thus the under 14 year old male was exempted from the offence since such a boy was presumed not to have attained puberty and was therefore incapable of emission of semen to lead to conception by the female. One can extend this argument to the requirement of the law that it will be rape only if the male sexual organ penetrates the female organ, for it is only then that procreation can occur.[8]

Who can be a victim?

Under the law, it is only a female person who can be a victim of rape. It has been argued by some that rape law should be sex neutral and protect any person from forced sexual intercourse as well as other sexual acts. The question is: Is it physically/ biologically possible to force a man to penetrate a woman's female organ, with his penis?

What is carnal knowledge?

The phrase 'carnal knowledge' means sexual intercourse; it refers to penetration of the male sexual organ into a woman's vagina. Thus if a man forcibly penetrates a woman's anus (*per anum*), or if he forcibly inserts any other object into her vagina or anus, or if he forces her to have fellatio (so called oral sex) with him or cunnilingus (touching the female sex organ with the lips and tongue), such conduct does not amount to rape although it may constitute other less serious offences such as indecent assault[9] or carnal knowledge against the order of nature.[10]

In *Uganda v Kyamusungu Ivan* Criminal Session Case No. 107/96 High Court, the accused was indicted for rape under Sections 117 and 118 of the Uganda Penal Code.

Held *inter alia*: Carnal knowledge means penetration of the male sexual organ into the female sexual organ. If there was no penetration then the offence of rape is not established.

In *Uganda v Odwong Dennis and Olanya Dickson* (1992-93) HCB 71 it was held *inter alia:*In rape cases the prosecution must prove penetration of the male reproductive organ into the female reproductive organ.

The use of euphemism

Victims and/or witnesses may be reluctant or unable to use correct anatomical terms to describe what has taken place. Courts have to decide if what they are describing constitutes an offence.

CASE: *Uganda v Tumuhirwe* Criminal Case No. 296/93 High Court

The accused was indicted for defilement (sexual intercourse with a girl under the age of 18) under Section 123 (1) (now 129) of the Uganda Penal Code. The complainant testified that on the relevant day, she was sleeping and woke up to find the accused on top of her. In the words of the complainant the accused had entered his *omukira* (tail) into her vagina.

Counsel for the accused argued *inter alia* that the complainant did not know what was used to defile her/she was doubtful as to whether she was actually defiled. She kept telling the court about *omukira*, which literally means tail, and yet human beings do not have tails.

Held by the court:

> It is true the complainant in her testimony informed the court that the man who defiled her used his tail but in the course of her testimony she clarified that by tail she meant that part of the body used by men when urinating. That explanation left no doubt that she was sexually intercoursed by a man using his penis.

Note: Although the accused appealed, the appeal was only against the sentence.

Slightest penetration is adequate

Several cases have clearly established that in a sexual offence based on sexual intercourse, the slightest penetration of the woman's vagina by the male organ is enough to constitute the offence and that emission of seed is not necessary.

CASE: *Muzeeyimana Phillipo v Uganda* Criminal Appeal No. 85/1999 Court of Appeal

The appellant was convicted of defilement. On appeal the defence counsel argued *inter alia* that the medical evidence submitted was inconclusive. There was no mention of penetration and that the discharge in the complainant's private parts did not contain any sperm. In his view there was no evidence of sexual intercourse having taken place.

Held: On appeal it was held *inter alia* that:

> Regarding the medical report, it is trite law that the slightest penetration is sufficient. This was manifested by the inflammation of the vestibule. The report states that such inflammation may usually follow an act of sexual intercourse. It is also well established that emission is not necessary for the offence to be established.

Ejaculation is not an ingredient in the offence of rape or defilement

CASE: *Uganda v Mugoya Wilson* Criminal Session Case No. 170/93 High Court[11]

The accused confessed that he did not ejaculate.

It was **held** *inter alia* that:

The slightest penetration is enough so it is not a defence to say that one just stopped at the mouth of the vagina, it is not also a defence to say that the accused did not ejaculate, because ejaculation is not one of the ingredients of the offence (Halsbury's Laws of England Volume 10, 3rd ed. para 1438 p. 746).

No need to prove rupture of the hymen by the accused or that the vagina was fully penetrated
CASES AND RULINGS

In *Uganda v Stephen Mulengera* (1994-95) HCB 28 it was stated that: 'There is no need for rupture of the hymen; the slightest penetration is enough.' (See also Court of Appeal decision in *Mukasa Evaristo v Uganda* Criminal Appeal 53/99.)

In *Uganda v Ddamulira Eriabu* Criminal Session Case No. 449/1995 it was stated that: 'Sexual intercourse is complete when the female organ is penetrated by the male sex organ; and it does not matter how slight such penetration may be. (See Archibold on *Criminal Pleadings, Evidence and Practice*, 38th ed., p.1124, para 2872.)

In *Uganda v Karimu Zawedde* Criminal Session Case No. 551/1996 High Court it was held *inter alia* that: 'In law sexual intercourse between a female and male human being is complete when the female's sexual organ is penetrated by the male's sexual organ. It is immaterial, though, how slight such penetration may be.' (see Archibold *Criminal Pleadings Evidence & Practice,* 38th ed., p. 2873 para 2872).

See also *Uganda v Baturine Richard* Criminal Session Case No. 589/1996 High Court where it was held that the slightest penetration was adequate to prove the case of defilement beyond reasonable doubt.

CASE: *Mukasa Everisto v Uganda* Criminal Appeal No. 53/99 Court of Appeal The appellant had been convicted of defilement under Section 123(1) and appealed *inter alia* against the conviction, arguing that there was no penetration because the doctor who examined the girl had found that the hymen had not been ruptured. [**Note**: the doctor who examined the victim confirmed that injuries found were compatible with sexual intercourse but that the hymen was not broken, i.e. the private parts were swollen and tender, the labia majora was swollen]. According to the defence counsel, the appellant should have been convicted of attempted defilement. The Court of Appeal confirmed the finding of the trial judge and said:

> It is trite law that penetration however slight will suffice to secure a conviction. The vagina need not be fully penetrated. It is enough for the evidence to show that there was entry of a male organ into the female organ. Proof of rupture of hymen is not necessary … As pointed out by the trial judge:

> 'Although her hymen was not broken there was penetration however slight. See *Uganda v Okello Francis*, Criminal Session Case No. 52/1992. See also *Uganda v Eddy Musasizi Turyahabwa* Criminal Session Case No. 75/1994 and in *Uganda v Mulengera* 1994-5 HCB 28 it was stated that no proof was needed to establish the rupture of the hymen as the very slightest penetration without rupturing the hymen by the penis of a man is sufficient in defilement.'

Result: Appeal dismissed.

Absence of the woman's consent is crucial in rape cases

It will be rape if a man has sexual intercourse with a female without her consent or with her consent if the consent is obtained by force or by means of threats or intimidation of any kind, or by fear of bodily harm, or by means of false representations as to the nature of the act, or in the case of a married woman, by impersonating her husband.[12]

Although a study of case law indicates that emphasis is usually placed on the use of force, it is clear from the section creating the offence that lack of consent is the crux of the matter and this may exist although no force is used. Thus the section creating the offence realises that a woman may *submit* to sexual intercourse as a result of threats and intimidation. That would not be consensual sex. A woman may also consent as a result of fraud and that again is not meaningful consent.

Thus in *Camplin* (1845) conviction was upheld where the defendant had sexual intercourse with a woman whom he had rendered insensible by giving her liquor.[13]

CASES AND RULINGS

In *Mayers* (1872) conviction was entered against a man who had sex with a woman who was asleep.

In *DPP v Morgan & 3 Others* [1976] AC 182 House of Lords, Lord Hailsham said *inter alia* that:

> Rape consists in having unlawful sexual intercourse with a woman without her consent and by force. … It does not mean there has to be a fight or blows have to be inflicted. It means there has to be some violence used against the woman to overbear her will or that there has to be a threat of violence as a result of which her will is overborne. (p. 208)

The law on rape punishes a man who through fraud/false representation gets the consent of the woman. The provision however is to the effect that the fraud must be to the *nature* of the act. Thus, where a woman who is completely ignorant of sexual matters, is persuaded to engage in sexual intercourse in the mistaken belief that this constitutes some other, beneficial conduct, such as medical treatment, such would constitute rape.

In *Williams* [1923] 1 KB 340 a conviction of rape was upheld where a singing master had sexual intercourse with a girl pupil by pretending that it was a method of improving her voice.

The question then is: if a woman who knows what constitutes sexual intercourse (i.e. the nature of the act) is persuaded to engage in sexual intercourse on a false representation as to its therapeutic effects, would such act be rape? Uganda's local newspapers are awash with instances of traditional medicine men who have sexual intercourse with female clients who go to them looking for a cure for the inability to have children. The medicine men tell their patients that through sexual intercourse with them, the women will be cured of barrenness. A woman in that situation would have consented to intercourse on the basis of a misrepresentation merely as to its qualities rather than its nature. In my opinion, such would not be rape. Such fraud does not go to the nature of the act.

CASE: *Nakholi v Republic* [1967] EA 337 Court of Appeal for East Africa
The appellant was convicted of rape. The complainant's age was taken by the trial

judge to be about 13 years but the medical officer's evidence was that her age ranged from 13 to 16 years. The judge in his address to the assessors and in his judgment stated that the question of the consent or otherwise of the complainant was not important as she was incapable at her age of giving consent. On appeal:

> Lack of consent is an essential ingredient in the proof of rape and although a girl may be of such tender age that mere proof of age is sufficient to establish lack of consent, this must be proved before convicting.

Note: Where an accused is indicted for the rape of an underage girl the ingredient of absence of consent must be proved. It is unwise for the prosecution to bring a charge of rape where it is obvious that the girl is under the minimum age of consent. The ingredient of absence of consent is not easy to prove. In a case of defilement all that the prosecution has to prove is sexual intercourse and the age of the child.[14] These are relatively easier to prove. However where the issue of age may be problematic, the prosecution should perhaps bring charges of rape and defilement as an alternative.

CASE: *Eria Ngobi* (1953) 20 EACA 154
The Court of Appeal for East Africa drew attention to the advisability, where it was clear that the girl was under the age limit, of bringing the charge under the section which makes it an offence to have carnal knowledge of a girl of that age rather than to bring a charge of rape where consent is a necessary element.

CASE: *Abudonio Alemo* (1953) 20 EACA 201
The Court of Appeal for East Africa pointed out the desirability in a charge of rape of adding a second count for defilement, where the complainant was under the age limit, in case the charge of rape broke down on the issue of consent.

Absence of consent is not synonymous with the use of force
A conviction of rape may be entered, though no evidence is tendered to show violence or resistance. Thus in *Fletcher* (1859)[15], the accused was convicted of raping a thirteen year old retarded girl who had not resisted his advances. Rejecting the contention, based on earlier authorities, that force was an essential element of the offence, Chief Justice Lord Campbell said at page 134:

> I am of the opinion that the conviction must be affirmed. The case has been very well argued. The definition of rape may now be considered *res adjudicata*. The question is, what is the proper definition of the crime of rape? Is it carnal knowledge of a woman against her will, or is it sufficient, if it be without the consent of the prosecutrix? If it must be against her will, then the crime was not proved in this case; but if the offence is complete where it was … without her consent, then the prisoner was properly convicted … The law, therefore, must now be taken to be settled, and ought not to be disturbed …

Lord Campbell also added:

> It would be monstrous to say that if a drunken woman returning from the market lay down and fell asleep by the roadside, and a man, by force, had connexion with her whilst she was in a state of insensibility and incapable of giving consent, he would not be guilty of rape.

Presence of injuries not part of ingredients of rape

CASE: *Oyeki Charles v Uganda* Criminal Appeal 126/1999 Court of Appeal for Uganda
Accused appealed against a conviction of rape. According to the learned counsel since the medical evidence revealed no injuries on the victim, prosecution had not proved forced sexual intercourse.

Held *inter alia* that the presence of injuries on the body of a woman alleging rape is not an ingredient of the offence. Court can convict in absence of injuries. What is necessary is proof of penetration and lack of consent.

The onus of proving lack of consent is on the prosecution

In all cases of rape, lack of consent is an issue.

CASE: *Kibazo v Uganda* [1965] EA 507 Court of Appeal for Eastern Africa.

In a charge of rape the onus is on the prosecution to prove that sexual intercourse took place without the consent of the complainant. The court should address its mind to the question of reasonable doubt on the issue of consent. The fact of non-consent must be proved to the satisfaction of the court. Court must be satisfied without reasonable doubt on the issue; otherwise there can be no conviction.

Mens rea of rape: Belief in consent is a defence

A man cannot be guilty of rape unless he knew at the time of the intercourse that it was against the woman's will or unless he had intercourse with her recklessly not caring whether she consented or not. The prosecution must show first and foremost that the woman did not consent and secondly that the man either knew that the woman was not consenting or did not care whether she consented or not.

Thus a man commits rape upon a woman if he has sexual intercourse with her without her consent and if at the time he knows that she is not consenting. The test applied to the man's mental element is a subjective test.

However unreasonable the accused's belief may seem, a man who honestly albeit mistakenly believes that the woman is consenting cannot be convicted of rape.

CASE: *DPP v Morgan & 3 Others* [1976] AC 182 House of Lords
The defendant M invited the other three defendants, much younger men, to his house and suggested that they should have intercourse with his wife. He told them that she was kinky and any apparent resistance on her part would be a mere pretence. Accordingly they did have intercourse with her, despite her struggles and protests. They were subsequently charged with rape and also together with M, with aiding and abetting rape. The wife gave evidence that she resisted and did not consent. The three men said they had believed what M had told them.

Held: That when a defendant had had sexual intercourse with a woman without her consent, genuinely believing nevertheless that she did consent, he was not to be convicted of rape, even though the jury were satisfied that he had no reasonable grounds for so believing.

- *Per* Lord Cross of Chelsea: A man who has intercourse with a woman, believing on inadequate grounds that she is consenting to it, does not commit rape in ordinary parlance or in law.

- *Per* Lord Hailsham of St Marylebone: In rape the prohibited act is intercourse without the consent of the victim and the mental element lies in the intention to commit the act willy-nilly or not caring whether the victim consents or not. A
  failure to prove this element involves an acquittal, because an essential ingredient is lacking and it matters not that it is lacking because of a belief not based on reasonable grounds.
- *Per* Lord Fraser of Tullybelton: If the effect of the evidence as a whole is that the defendant believed or may have believed that the victim was consenting, the prosecution has not discharged the onus of proving commission of the offence and no question can arise as to whether the belief was reasonable or not, though the reasonableness or otherwise of the belief is important as evidence tending to show whether the belief was truly held.

It can therefore be concluded that in a prosecution for rape the following must be proved:
- Intercourse
- Absence of consent
- Knowledge by the accused of absence of consent or indifference as to its existence.

The majority position in Morgan was later codified by Section 1 of England's Sexual Offences (Amendment) Act 1976. But should the law not apply the test of a reasonable man and thus ask the question: would a reasonable person (man) have believed that the victim was consenting?

Despite the above position of the law as elucidated by the majority view of the House of Lords in Morgan's case, it is valuable to cite an observation by one of the dissenting judges – Lord Simon. In his opinion the law should require that the belief of the accused should be *reasonably* held. As to why the law should so require, Lord Simon said:

> The policy of the law in this regard could well derive from its concern to hold a fair balance between victim and accused. It would hardly seem just to fob off a victim of a savage assault with such comfort as he could derive from knowing that his injury was caused by a belief, however absurd, that he was about to attack the accused. A respectable woman who has been ravished would hardly feel that she was vindicated by being told that her assailant must go unpunished because he believed, quite unreasonably, that she was consenting to sexual intercourse with him.

There are groups who argue for a stricter position than that put forward by Lord Simon. They argue that liability for rape should be imposed where in fact the woman did not consent, regardless of whether the accused could reasonably have been aware of this fact. Such groups argue that it is so important that a woman should not be subjected to sexual intercourse without her consent that men should be required to ensure, at their peril, that they obtain that consent. It is contended that if men find the prospect of fulfilling this task too onerous, they are free to abstain from sexual relations.[16] Liability would thus depend on whether or not the woman in *fact* consented, and not on the man's mental state. I however note that the above argument would go against the basic principle of criminal law that a person should only be liable for a crime where he/she has a guilty mind.

Unlawful sexual intercourse and marriage

Sexual intercourse without the woman's consent will only be unlawful if it is outside marriage. The law exempts a husband from the offence of raping his wife.

In *Clarence* (1888) 22 QBD at 51 Justice Hawkins said that the consent of the wife is given on marriage and is irrevocable. As far back as the seventeenth century, Hale wrote:

> The husband cannot be guilty of a rape committed upon his lawful wife, for by their mutual matrimonial consent and contract the wife hath given up herself in this kind unto her husband, which she cannot retract.[17]

A husband can be guilty of physical assault if he inflicts injury on wife in order to have sexual intercourse with her

CASE: *Miller v R* [1954] All ER 529

The accused had forceful sexual intercourse with his wife. She suffered injuries. It was held that a husband could not be guilty of raping his wife. At marriage the wife consents to the husband exercising marital rights of sexual intercourse. The judge observed that during intercourse the ordinary relations created by marriage subsist between the spouses. Sexual intercourse is therefore not by special consent but is an obligation imposed upon a wife during the subsistence of a marriage. The accused was only found guilty of assault occasioning actual bodily harm.

It is argued by many that a prosecution for marital rape would destroy the unity of the family, promote marital disharmony and hamper attempts at reconciliation.[18]

It has also been argued that it would be very difficult to prove marital rape and thus the law should not recognise it. In other words it is said that evidential problems which are already enormous in sexual assaults between unmarried parties would be even more complex in cases involving wife/husband accusations. I am however in agreement with the Ireland Law Reform Commission in its October 1987 Consultation paper on Rape where it is said:

> We do not see the difficulty of proof as a reason for retaining the exemption. We consider it anomalous that a prosecution should be prevented on that basis when it is permitted in cases of non-marital cohabitation, where the evidential difficulties would be similar. Moreover, similar difficulties of proof may arise in assault proceedings involving husbands and wives. They are quite rightly not regarded as a reason for prohibiting such proceedings.[19]

In her defence of the continuation of marriage as a defence in a rape trial Okagbue[20] argued that it is only in exceptional circumstances that the criminal law should invade the bedroom. In other words the writer invokes public policy to support the retention of the defence.

Onalenna Selolwane (2003)[21] reacted to the defence of a marital relationship in marriage in Botswana thus:

> There is a prevailing myth that is often perpetuated by people unskilled in the art and craft of consensual intercourse that somehow men need to use force to get sexual compliance from women. This myth leads to [people] assuming that the criminalization of sexual violence within marriage would therefore lead to rape being the 'most prevalent

and pervasive offence in any court'. But the majority of men are not brutish animals. As those who have gained mastery of the sexual geography of the female body and the functions of the various parts can attest, they never have to use force to gain the kind of sexual gratification that consensual sex has to offer. A woman who persistently refuses the sexual advances of her husband or partner is a woman who is tired of unfulfilling quickies or a diet of coercive humps that are devoid of exploration and discovery. The proper remedy is basic sexual lessons, not the legal sanctioning of brutality.

A husband can be convicted for aiding and abetting the rape of his wife

CASE: *DPP v Morgan & 3 Others* [1976] AC 182 House of Lords

In Morgan's case although he had sexual intercourse with his wife without her consent, he could not be charged with rape. However, he was charged with aiding three other men in raping his wife.

Exceptions

An exception to the rule that a man cannot be guilty of raping his wife is that if divorce proceedings have been instituted in a court of law and a decree *nisi* has been pronounced, a man can be found guilty of rape if he has sexual intercourse with his wife without her consent.

The exception also applies in cases where a lawful separation order which contains a non-molestation clause has been pronounced by a court of law. In the English case of *Clarke*, the wife had obtained a non-cohabitation order from the justices which had the 'effect in all respects of a decree of judicial separation' from her husband, on account of his persistent cruelty. It could be discharged if she committed adultery or voluntarily resumed cohabitation with her husband. The husband was charged with raping her at a time after the order was made. A motion to quash the court order on the ground that it did not disclose any offence known to the law failed. Justice Byrne accepted that 'as a general proposition' a husband could not be guilty of rape on his wife. Echoing Hale, he observed that the marital right of the husband existed by virtue of the consent given by the wife at the time of the marriage and not by virtue of a consent given at the time of each act of intercourse as in the case of unmarried persons. 'Thus,' he said, 'the intercourse is not by virtue of any special consent, but is based on an obligation imposed on the wife by reason of the marriage.' However, in the present case, the position was that:

> The wife, by process of law, namely, by marriage, had given consent to the husband to exercise the marital right during such time as the ordinary relations created by the marriage contract subsisted between them, but by a further process of law, namely, the justices' order, her consent to marital intercourse was revoked. Thus in my opinion, the husband was not entitled to have intercourse with her without her consent.[22]

It should be noted that the English common law position on marital rape as enunciated above is being departed from in several jurisdictions, although in Uganda the issue has never been brought before a court of law. In Scotland for example a man can be found guilty of raping his wife. In *HM Advocate v Duffy* (1989) SLT 469, HC of Just, the accused person was indicted for assault and rape of his wife. At the time of the assault the two were living apart although no decree of judicial separation had been pronounced.

Lord Robertson observed that the whole position of marriage and the status of women today is different from what it was in the past. If a man could be found guilty in whatever way and degree of seriousness of violence against his wife, it would be unreasonable not to find him guilty of rape of the same wife if the necessary facts were proved. The court held that the marital exemption, if it had ever been a part of the law of Scotland, was no longer so.

CASE: In *R v R* [1991] 4 All ER 481 Lord Keith, on behalf of the Law Lords held that the common law was 'capable of evolving in the light of changing social, economic and cultural developments.' He continued:

> Hale's proposition reflected the state of affairs in these respects at the time it was enunciated. Since then the status of women, and particularly of married women, has changed out of all recognition in various ways which are very familiar and upon which it is unnecessary to go into detail. Apart from property matters and the availability of matrimonial remedies, one of the most important changes is that *marriage is in modern times regarded as a partnership of equals,* and no longer one in which the wife must be the subservient chattel of the husband. Hale's proposition involves that by marriage a wife gives her irrevocable consent to sexual intercourse with her husband under all circumstances and irrespective of the state of her health or how she happens to be feeling at the time. In modern times any reasonable person must regard that conception as quite unacceptable. (My emphasis)

In *Reg v R* (1992) 1 AC 612 the House of Lords rejected the presumption of consent to sexual intercourse as an anachronism and offensive.

---

1. Originally Section 117.
2. Originally Section 118.
3. Section 9 (1) of the Uganda Penal Code: When an offence is committed, each of the following persons is deemed to have taken part in committing the offence and to be guilty of the offence, and may be charged with actually committing it, that is to say a) every person who actually does the act or makes the omission which constitutes the offence b) every person who does or omits to do any act for the purpose of enabling or aiding another person to to commit the offence c) every person who aids or abets another person in the committing of the offence.
4. *R. v Groombridge* (1836) 173 ER 256
5. *R. v Phillips* (1839) 8 C & O 736
6. *Women, Race and Class*, Vintage Books, NY
7. See McCriff 'Reform of Sexual Offences in Victoria: The Time to Abandon Victorian Perspective' (1980) 4 Crim LJ 328 328
8. Refer to the legal meaning of carnal knowledge/sexual intercourse discussed below.
9. Section 128 of the Penal Code.
10. Section 145 of the Penal Code.
11. Confirmed by the Court of Appeal. Although the case went to the Supreme Court on further appeal the holdings mentioned here were not overturned.
12. *R v Case* (1850), 169 ER 381 R v Dee (1884), 15 Cox CC 579.

13. 1 Den. 89, 169 ER 163.
14. The offence of defilement is discussed in detail later.
15. 8 Cox CC 131
16. See for example some arguments quoted by the Ireland Law Reform Commission in its October 1987 Consultation Paper on Rape. Page 85 of 171. http://www.lawreform.ie/publications/data/volume6/lrc-42.html. Accessed on 15-06-2004.
17. Quoted in Freeman M.D.A. 'Rape By a Husband' in *New Journal* vol. 129 April 1979.
18. See for example Freeman ibid.
19. http://www.lawreform.ie/publications/data/volume6/lrc-42.html. Page 80 of 171. accessed on 15-06-2004.
20. 'The Reform of Sexual Offences in Nigerian Criminal Law' in Nigerian Institute of Advanced Legal Studies, 1991 at 6.
21. 'Talking Gender and Development.' Mmegi Monitor 43, 16th August 2003.
22. [1949] 2 All ER 448.

3
Attempted Rape and Indecent Assault

Attempt to commit rape: Section 125 of the Uganda Penal Code Act.[1]

Section 125 of the Uganda Penal Code provides that any person who attempts to commit rape commits a felony. It is also provided that a person guilty under the section is liable to imprisonment for life with or without corporal punishment. However, in *Kyamanywa Simon v Uganda*[2], the Constitutional Court declared the use of corporal punishment on anybody who has been convicted of an offence, unconstitutional for violating a person's right to protection from cruel, inhuman and degrading treatment. Consequently Ugandan Courts can no longer sentence a person to corporal punishment.

CASE: *Achoki v Republic* EALR [200] 2 EA 283 Court of Appeal for Kenya
Evidence was accepted by the trial magistrate and confirmed by the High Court that the appellant accosted the complainant, knocked her down, tore away her knickers and lay on top of her. He was at the same time lowering his own trousers and he tried to get in between her thighs. The complainant was all the time screaming and her screams brought Prosecution Witness 2 on the scene. The latter testified that he found the appellant lying on top of the complainant.

The appellant was charged on a count of attempted rape with an alternative count of indecent assault. The particulars of the charge were that the accused had 'attempted to have carnal knowledge of the victim.' On appeal to the Court of Appeal of Kenya, it was held:

- The particulars of the offence of attempted rape must state that the attempted carnal knowledge was unlawful and without consent.
- It is lack of consent which makes the act of carnal knowledge unlawful. Whether the charge be one of rape or attempted rape the particulars must state that the attempted unlawful carnal knowledge was without consent of the woman or girl.
- The facts apart from supporting a charge of attempted rape, which charge as already said was incurably defective, also supported the alternative charge of indecent assault.

Indecent Assault: Sections 128[3] and 147[4] of the Uganda Penal Code Act

Indecent assault occurs when an assault is accompanied by messages with sexual connotations. The message may be verbal or through gestures and/or other actions. In addition, where an accused is indicted for rape the trial court has power to return a verdict of either indecent assault or of defilement. See *Nakholi v Republic* [1967] EA 337 Court of Appeal for East Africa. And in *Eria Ngobi v R* (1953) 20 EACA 154 (U) it was held that 'Upon an indictment of rape contrary to Section 117 of the Penal Code the accused may be convicted of indecent assault contrary to Section 122 of the Code.'

Under Section 128 (1) of the Uganda Penal Code, it is an offence to unlawfully and indecently assault a woman or a girl.

Section 128 (2) provides that where the female is under the age of 18 years, consent to the act is not a defence.

Section 147 provides that any person who unlawfully and indecently assaults a boy under the age of 18 years is guilty of a crime.

It is noted that the victim of an indecent assault is either a female or a male. Where the victim is a female (Section 128), she can be an adult female, i.e. above 18 years, or a female under the age of 18 years. What makes the conduct unlawful in the case of an adult female would be that the accused is not her husband and also that the conduct complained of was unwanted. Where the female victim is under the age of 18 years, consent is not a defence. Just as in the case of defilement of a girl under the age of 18 years, the law presumes that a girl under 18 years is not capable of giving meaningful consent to sexual behaviour. The law recognises that a male child, i.e. under 18 years of age, can be indecently assaulted but is silent on an adult male.

CASE: *Hamisi v R* [1972] EA 367 High Court of Tanzania
The complainant was walking home. The accused who was riding a bike overtook her and after riding a few steps ahead alighted from his bike and appeared as if he was repairing his bicycle. When the complainant reached him the accused threw his bike to the ground and held the complainant and said to her that he was going to have sexual intercourse with her by force. According to the evidence, the accused then dragged her to a place where there was tall grass and threw her to the ground, drew a knife and threatened to kill her if she did not comply with his request. According to her evidence the accused holding the knife at her, forced her to remove her underclothes, which she did. The accused then started to remove his trousers but as he was doing so a police car stopped nearby and the complainant called for help. The driver of the car went to the scene and took both parties to the police station.

Accused was charged with attempted rape but the trial magistrate found him guilty of indecent assault.
Held on Appeal: An assault becomes indecent if it is accompanied by utterances suggestive of sexual intercourse.

Judgement:

> TheTrial Magistrate was right in holding that a charge of attempted rape was unsupportable. An assault on a lady though not indecent in itself becomes indecent if it is accompanied by indecent utterances suggestive of sexual intercourse. As the accused in this case had earlier asked the complainant to have sexual intercourse with him and he, in trying to accomplish his passions, threw her to the ground, his throwing her to the ground amounted to indecent assault. The forcing by the accused of the complainant to remove her underpants amounted to removing the underpants of the complainant by the accused. The accused as such was guilty of indecent assault.

1. Originally Section 119.
2. Constitutional Ref. No. 10 of 2000
3. Originally Section 122.
4. Originally Section 142.

4
The Rape Trial

The three basic ingredients which the prosecution must prove in a rape case are vaginal penetration by the penis (carnal knowledge), the lack of consent by the complainant and that it was the accused who in fact committed the crime. See *Katumba James v Uganda* Criminal Appeal No. 45/1999 Supreme Court.

Burden of proof

In line with the criminal principle that a person is innocent until proved guilty, the onus of proving each ingredient lies squarely on the prosecution and the standard must be beyond reasonable doubt. This onus never shifts. In *Uganda v Moses Bagada* Criminal Case No. 98/90 the High Court restated this principle and said:

> The accused (in a rape case) has no duty to prove his innocence even if his defence is disbelieved. Where he puts up an alibi … he does not assume the duty of proving it. It suffices if he manages to raise some doubt in the court's mind.

Suggested reform: Whereas the prosecution should prove its case beyond reasonable doubt as with other criminal cases, such burden should be lightened by shifting the onus of proof to the accused every time he erects a defence in his favour. Thus if he pleads an alibi he must proceed to prove it. (Tamale).

How is rape proved? Proof of sexual intercourse

Proof that sexual intercourse actually took place may be by:
1. Testimony of the victim
2. Testimony of other witnesses:
- Who saw the act
- Who the woman reported the assault to
- Medical evidence, e.g. fluids from the man's body found in the woman's body or clothes

Proof of sexual intercourse: absence of medical evidence not fatal

CASE: *Oyeki Charles v Uganda* Criminal Appeal No. 126/1999 Court of Appeal for Uganda

The appellant was convicted of rape. Brief facts of the case were that while the complainant (Nanyonga) was walking behind her daughter (Nakayima) along a village path, the appellant grabbed her, threw her down and forcibly had sexual intercourse with her. She raised an alarm which drew the attention of Nakayima who turned and saw the appellant on top of her mother having sexual intercourse with her. Nakayima ran to her brother Katongole who came back to the scene and pulled the appellant from their mother.

Counsel for the appellant argued that the element of sexual intercourse had not been proved beyond reasonable doubt. That the medical evidence of the doctor who examined the victim was not sufficient to corroborate her testimony. According to the learned counsel the evidence revealed no injuries on the victim to prove forced sexual intercourse. He further criticised the evidence of the police woman who claimed to have examined the victim and found semen in the area of the victim's private parts. Counsel submitted that the evidence was worthless to prove sexual intercourse because the policewoman is not an expert.

On the other hand the state attorney contended that there was sufficient evidence to prove sexual intercourse. It was argued that for the ingredient of sexual intercourse, the trial judge did not rely on the medical evidence as the examination was carried out on the victim 2 weeks after the event when all evidence of sexual intercourse would have been lost. According to the state attorney the trial judge relied on the evidence of the victim and of her daughter who witnessed the sexual act. It was argued that the trial judge was entitled to believe these witnesses if she found them truthful.

The Court of Appeal **held** *inter alia*:

> Medical evidence is certainly the best evidence to prove sexual intercourse but it is by no means the only one. Other cogent evidence could also do.

> The trial judge was justified in basing her judgement on the evidence of the two witnesses (the victim and the eyewitness) that sexual intercourse had been proved beyond reasonable doubt.

> The evidence was also adequate to prove that the sexual intercourse was without the victim's consent. He grabbed her from behind, threw her down when his trousers were already removed and had sexual intercourse with her.

Proof of penetration without medical evidence

It is possible to prove penetration without adducing medical evidence. It can be proved through the testimony of the victim.

CASE: *Katumba James v Uganda* Criminal Appeal No. 58/97 Court of Appeal
The appellant was convicted of rape contrary to Sections 117 and 118 of the Uganda Penal Code. He appealed against conviction.

On 8 March 1997 the complainant was walking along a village path through a forest when she saw the appellant following her. He called her and asked her to stop. She refused. He then ran after her, caught up with her, grabbed her and threw her down. He then dragged her to a spot about 3 metres from the path and raped her while she raised an alarm. The alarm was answered by PW2 who found the appellant lying on top of the complainant and having sex with her. On seeing PW2 the appellant ran away. The complainant was examined by a medical doctor who did not testify because he was not present on the day the prosecution chose to close its case.

On the issue of penetration, the Court of Appeal **held**:

> There can be no doubt that there was penetration, notwithstanding that no medical evidence was led on the point. The complainant was an old woman of 40 years. She had 9 children. It was her evidence that the appellant inserted his penis in her vagina and accomplished the sexual act twice before PW2 arrived at the scene. It was her evidence that when PW2 arrived the appellant's penis was still inside her vagina. She must have known what she was talking about.

Result: Appeal dismissed..

How is rape proved? Absence of consent

Proof that the victim did not consent to sexual intercourse with the accused may be by:
- Testimony of the victim
- Evidence of a struggle
- The state of the victim when she first reported the assault.

It is not part of the element of rape that the victim should have injuries. What is necessary is proof of penetration and lack of consent.

CASE: *Kayondo Robert v Uganda* Criminal Appeal No. 18/96 Court of Appeal

The appellant had been convicted of rape. According to the complainant she had on the night of the crime opened the door of her house in answer to a call by the appellant who was her nephew. While standing at the door she had held a conversation with him until she said she was tired and wanted to go to bed. The appellant had then grabbed her neck, pushed her inside the house and had sexual intercourse with her without her consent. Because she was being held by the neck she could not make an alarm. She was overwhelmed and she removed her clothes as ordered by the appellant.

The complainant was examined by a doctor three days later and marks of violence were found on the neck. In the doctor's view the marks were consistent with struggle. However there was no evidence on her private parts to indicate forcible sexual intercourse.

On appeal the Court of Appeal noted that the trial judge gave consideration to the fact that it could not have been possible for the doctor to find any signs of forcible intercourse since the complainant had been married and had three children and was at the time of the offence pregnant.

The Court of Appeal then added:
- We would only add that though rape has high evidentiary requirements courts are sometimes willing to draw inference based on circumstances.
- The justification for stiff requirement is the danger of false accusations.
- Penetration as the judge found can be proved by circumstantial evidence.
- The complainant claimed to have been 'forced', the word force has no other signification than that the appellant accomplished the sexual intercourse sought by him without the victim's consent.
- The fact that the complainant removed her clothes was no evidence that she consented. She did so because she feared the accused would kill her if she refused.
- The injuries found on the complainant's body were clearly evidence of struggle.
- The nature of inconsistencies regarding the trend of events during the struggle (e.g. which items of clothes she put off first, etc.) were not fundamental. Involuntary sex was in itself a traumatic experience and it would be most unlikely for the complainant to mentally register the exact sequence of events as they occurred. The sequence is not important as it does not go to the actual act of sexual intercourse or to the identity of the appellant.
- Uncorroborated evidence of the complainant would be considered insufficient to base a conviction on if it contained numerous and serious contradictions.

Consent and the complainant's character

At common law the accused in a rape trial is allowed to adduce evidence of previous consenting sexual relations between himself and the victim, on the ground that such evidence makes it more likely that the victim consented on the occasion in question. MacFarlane in his *Historical Development of the Offence of Rape*[1] reports that at the beginning of the nineteenth century, Archbold linked the complainant's occupation as a prostitute with the issue of her credibility on the witness stand thus:

> ... such circumstances should certainly operate with the jury as to the credibility of the fact, that connection was had with the woman against her consent.

Thus in *R v Clarke* (1817)[2], Justice Holroyd held that general evidence could be called to show that the woman was a prostitute because it tended to establish that intercourse took place with consent.

Uganda's Section 154 (d) of the Evidence Act[3] provides that:

> The credit of a witness may be impeached in the following ways by the adverse party:

> – when a man is prosecuted for rape or an attempt to ravish, by evidence that the prosecutrix was of generally immoral character.

The effect of Section 154 of the Evidence Act is to allow the defence to question the complainant on her past conduct/previous sexual experiences even with people other than the accused. The aim of such questions is to impugn the character of the complainant. Where the accused's defence is a belief in consent, evidence that she did not discriminate in her choice of sexual partners helps the defence case. It throws doubt on her assertion that she did not consent on the basis that such a woman would be more likely to have agreed to the act which the accused is being charged with. *It can thus be contended that rape is an offence, perhaps the only offence wherein the victim is treated like an accused.*

MacFarlane (*op cit*) asks a most pertinent question: How does lack of chastity become relevant to the material issue of consent and the collateral issue of credibility in a rape trial? He rightly questions the assumption inherent in Section 154 that women who have had sexual relations with several men are more inclined, firstly to be untruthful, and, secondly, to consent to sexual relations in a wide variety of circumstances.

Several courts have also challenged such beliefs. In *R v Gun; ex parte* Stephenson[4] (South Australian Supreme Court) Chief Justice Bray said in 1977:

> I find it hard to believe that any reasonable person at the present time could assent to any of the following absurd propositions:
> 1. That a willingness to have sexual intercourse outside marriage with someone is equivalent to a willingness to have sexual intercourse outside marriage with anyone.
> 2. That the unchaste are also liable to be untruthful.
> 3. That a woman who has had sexual intercourse outside marriage is a fallen woman and deserves any sexual fate that comes her way.

In 1991 the Supreme Court of Canada made the following remarks in the case of *R v Seaboyer*[5]:

In my opinion evidence of prior acts of prostitution or allegations of prostitution is never relevant and besides its irrelevance, is highly prejudicial. I vehemently disagree with the assertion that a prostitute is generally more willing to consent to sexual intercourse and is less credible as a witness because of that mode of life. (Justice L'Heureux-Dube)

Evidence of struggle may prove absence of consent

CASE: *Kyamusungu Ivan v Uganda* Criminal Appeal No. 67/1998 Court of Appeal
The appellant was convicted of rape under Sections 117 and 118 of the Uganda Penal Code. He appealed on proof of absence of consent. The Court of Appeal agreed with the finding of the High Court and said *inter alia*:

> The complainant was examined by a doctor whose evidence was that the complainant had had sexual intercourse, had sustained injuries on the thighs, legs, and elbow, and that she had inflammation around her private parts. In his opinion the injuries were consistent with her having put up a struggle with the person who had sexual intercourse with her. That evidence clearly supported the complainant's claim that she had not consented to the sexual act and that the appellant had man handled her and injured her in the course of the rape. The medical report negatived consent.

Result: Appeal dismissed.

CASE: *Uganda v James Katumba* Criminal Session Case No. 333/97 High Court
In concluding that there was absence of consent to sexual intercourse, the judge was guided by the following facts:
1. The accused pulled the complainant to the scene where he had sexual intercourse with her. This was a sign that the complainant did not consent to the act of sexual intercourse.
2. The complainant made an alarm and this was an indicator that she did not approve of the sexual intercourse. (The alarm was answered by 2 people who found the accused on top of the woman.)
3. When the police visited the scene of the alleged offence, there were sign of struggle.
4. When the alarm was answered, the accused jumped off from the woman and ran away. This was taken as a sign of guilt.

On appeal (*Katumba James v Uganda* Criminal Appeal No. 58/97 Court of Appeal) the appeal court held *inter alia* 'Like the trial judge, we are satisfied that the complainant did not, indeed could not, consent since she was dragged to the scene of crime and raised an alarm throughout her ordeal. In any case, she had consented there would have been no need for the appellant to run away on seeing the people who answered the alarm since the complainant was not married and so could have sex with whoever she chose.'

Absence of signs of struggle may lead to acquittal

CASE: *Uganda v Makooba* Criminal Session Case No. 55/1999
The court **held**:

> If the accused and Makumbi had raped her while she struggled then there must have been bruises and perhaps scratches around her thighs. There were none at all ... Thus

it seems that if she did have sexual intercourse on that day, it must have taken place without any struggling or force used.

Similar conclusions were arrived at in *Uganda v Tumwesigye* Criminal Session Case No. 40/1990. The High Court said:

> On being examined by the doctor, no injuries consistent with force were found on her.

It was thus concluded by the court that it had not been proved beyond reasonable doubt that the sexual intercourse was non-consensual.

How is rape proved? Identification of the accused

The third ingredient which the prosecution must prove in a rape case is that the person accused was the one who actually committed the crime. This can be established by:
- Testimony of the victim
- Testimony of witnesses who saw accused and victim together
- Medical evidence, e.g. fluids of the man found in the woman's body
- Conduct of the accused

In many criminal cases the issue at stake rotates around the identity of the alleged accused persons. In a sexual offence like rape or defilement, just as in any other criminal cases, the accused may put up an alibi. In other words he completely denies the offence and states that he was not even at the scene of the alleged crime at the relevant time: he was elsewhere. Appeals against conviction are often on the ground that whereas the accused put up an alibi, the prosecution did not disprove the alibi beyond reasonable doubt.

In cases where the accused was identified by a single witness, the defence often challenges the ability of the single witness in accurately identifying the accused as the person who committed the crime. The cases which follow discuss how courts have resolved the issue of identity in general and the rules established are applicable even in cases of sexual assaults.

CASE: *Uganda v Kyamusungu Ivan* Criminal Session Case No. 107/96
The accused was indicted for rape under Sections 117 and 118 of the Uganda Penal Code.
Held *inter alia*: The accused must be connected to the commission of the offence by evidence pointing to positive identification of him as the assailant. Factors to be taken into account to establish identification have been laid down as follows:
1. Whether the accused was known to the complainant.
2. The time the incident took place.
3. The time the accused was under observation.
4. The distance between the accused and witnesses.

In other words, the circumstances under which the offence was committed must favour correct identification.
Note: On appeal to the Court of Appeal for Uganda, the appeal was dismissed, see *Kyamusungu Ivan v Uganda* Criminal Appeal No. 67/98.

CASE: *Kato Sula v Uganda* Criminal Appeal No. 30/1999 Court of Appeal
The accused was convicted of defiling a pupil in the school where he was a teacher.
The only eyewitness to the sexual intercourse was the victim. In regard to the issue of
identification the court **held**:

> The complainant knew her assaulter well before the offence, the assaulter spent a lot of
> time talking to her before and after the defilement ...These conditions favoured correct
> identification of the accused.

CASE: *Uganda v Godfrey Agudi* Criminal Session Case No 02/97 (defilement)
The court *inter alia* held that in ascertaining whether or not the accused was properly
identified, the court is required to take into account such factors as whether the witness
knew the accused before the incident, the time when the incident is alleged to have
taken place, the length of time and opportunity the witness took observing the accused
and the distance between the two. (See *Uganda v Wilson Simbwa* Supreme Court
Criminal Appeal No. 37/95)

CASE: In *Ntambi Francis v Uganda* Criminal Appeal No. 19/98 the Court of Appeal
cited with approval *Abdala Nabudere v Uganda* (1979) HCB 77 where it was stated
that in deciding whether or not a witness was able to identify his attacker, the court had
to take into account such matters as the source of light, whether or not the victim knew
the attacker before, the distance between the attacker and the victim, and the time the
victim took observing the attacker.

CASE: *Ochit Lagol v Uganda* Court of Appeal of Uganda Criminal Appeal No.21/97
The appellant was convicted of rape and aggravated robbery. He appealed *inter alia*
on the ground that the trial judge erred in law and in fact in holding that the appellant
had been positively identified when the circumstances did not favour correct identification.
It was argued that it was raining and the burning grass could not possibly have emitted
bright light to enable proper identification of the appellant. There were several gunshots
which were fired at the victims during the attack. This could have frightened the victims
and impaired their minds so that they were not in a position to positively identify the
appellant. In those circumstances the identification was not free from the possibility of
error.

The Court cited with approval the following passage from *Abdala bin Wendo v R*
[1953] 20 EACA also cited in *Roria v Republic* [1967]:

> Subject to certain well-known exceptions, it is trite that a fact may be proved by the
> testimony of a single witness but this rule does not lessen the need for testing with the
> greatest care the evidence of a single witness respecting identification especially when
> it is known that conditions favouring a correct identification were difficult. In such
> circumstances what is needed is the other evidence whether it be circumstantial or
> direct, pointing to guilt from which a judge can reasonably conclude that the evidence of
> identification, although based on the testimony of a single witness can safely be accepted
> as free from the possibility of error.

The test for accepting evidence of identification is therefore freedom from possibility
of error.

The court then pointed out the following factors as factors which favoured proper identification:

- The burning grass gave sufficient light.
- The incident lasted for two hours and the witnesses were close to the attackers.
- The witnesses knew the appellant before the incident.
- On reporting the incident the following morning the witness named the appellant as one of the attackers.

Identification of accused: evidence of a single witness

It is legally possible to convict on the uncorroborated evidence of a single witness.

CASE: *Roria v Republic* [1967] EA 583 Court of Appeal for East Africa.
In a case which rests mainly on the evidence of a single witness the court has to satisfy itself that the witness was not mistaken in her identification and that in all circumstances it is safe to act on such identification. Once satisfied, court can convict on the evidence of a single witness.

The court observed that:

> A conviction resting entirely on identity causes a degree of uneasiness ... that danger is, of course, greater when the only evidence against an accused person is identification by one witness and although no one would suggest that a conviction based on such identification should never be upheld it is the duty of this court to satisfy itself that in all the circumstances it is safe to act on such identification.

The court then quoted with approval *Abdala bin Wendo v R* (20 EACA at 168):

> Subject to certain well-known exceptions it is trite law that a fact may be proved by the testimony of a single witness but this rule does not lessen the need for testing with the greatest care the evidence of a single witness respecting identification, especially when it is known that the conditions favouring a correct identification were difficult. In such circumstances what is needed is other evidence, whether it be circumstantial or direct, pointing to guilt, from which a judge or jury can reasonably conclude that the evidence of identification, although based on the testimony of a single witness, can safely be accepted as free from the possibility of error.

A witness may be honest but mistaken.

The accused's alibi

In the celebrated case of *Woolmington v DPP* (1935) AC 462 it was held that there is no burden of proof on an accused who puts forward an alibi. He merely has to raise it.

CASES AND RULINGS

In *Uganda v Swaibu Kyabe* Criminal Session Case No. 427/96 High Court: An accused person has no obligation to prove an alibi. It is for the prosecution to destroy the alibi. (*Ssekitoleko v Uganda* [1967] EA 53). The prosecution destroys an accused's alibi by placing the accused at the scene of the crime.

In *Uganda v John O. Okong* Criminal Session Case No. 124/74: It is trite law that an accused person who puts forward an alibi as a defence to a criminal charge does not thereby assume the burden of proving the defence. *Aniseth v R* [1963] EA266

In *Muhammad Mukasa & Another v Uganda* Criminal Appeal No. 27/95 Supreme Court: It is settled law that where an accused person puts forward an alibi as an answer to a charge, he does not assume any burden of proving that answer. The burden to disprove the alibi is on the prosecution by placing the accused at the scene of crime.

CASE: *Remegious Kiwanuka v Uganda* Criminal Appeal No. 41/95 Supreme Court
In a defilement case a teacher was alleged to have defiled his student. The teacher denied the offence and put forward an alibi. The Supreme Court stated:

> The appellant was a teacher at the school where the complainant was a pupil. She knew him well and the incident took place in broad day light. The conditions were, therefore favourable to correct identification. The complainant's testimony contained a detailed account of what happened from the time the appellant sent her to buy sugar and how she was ravaged by the appellant ...

Court found that the trial court and the Court of Appeal was justified in accepting the complainant's evidence as truthful and rejecting the appellant's defence of alibi as having been negatived by the complainant's evidence.

---

1. http:/canadiancriminallaw.com/articles/toc/Hist- Dev- Rape – toc.htm. Accessed on 14 June 2004.
2. 2 Stark 241; 171 ER 633.
3. Chapter 6 Laws of Uganda (Revised Edition, 2000).
4. Cited in Bruce A. MacFarlane *supra*
5. Cited in Bruce A. MacFarlane *ibid*

The need for corroboration in sexual offences

Under common law the evidence of a complainant in a sexual offence[1] must be corroborated with either direct or indirect circumstantial evidence. Every judge must warn herself/himself and the assessors of the danger of convicting an accused person on the uncorroborated evidence of the complainant in a sexual offence.[2]

CASE: *Remegious Kiwanuka v Uganda* Criminal Appeal No. 41/1995
The Supreme Court held that it is settled law that in sexual offences, though corroboration of the prosecution evidence is not essential in law, it is in practice always looked for, and it is the established practice to warn the assessors against the danger of acting upon uncorroborated testimony.

What is corroboration?

Corroboration is independent evidence which supports the testimony of the complainant: confirmation from some other source that the witness (complainant) is telling the truth in some part of her story which goes to show that the accused committed the offence. Corroboration is not confirmation by independent evidence of everything said by the complainant. What is required is some independent evidence which implicates the accused in some material particular, tending to show that not only the offence has been committed, but also that it has been committed by the accused. This can be the testimony of other witnesses, it can be circumstantial evidence.

Corroborative evidence may be direct or circumstantial

According to John Burke's Osborne's *Concise Dictionary*, corroboration is independent evidence which implicates a person accused of a crime by connecting him with it. It is evidence which confirms in some material particular not only that the crime was committed but also that it was the accused who committed it.

In *Katumba James v Uganda* Criminal Appeal 45/1999 Supreme Court the court defined corroboration as follows:

> Corroboration is additional independent evidence which connects the accused with the crime, confirming in some material particulars not only the evidence that the crime has been committed, but also that the accused has committed it. Corroboration is in relation to the offence as a whole.

The court must explain its position on corroboration

In *Uganda v Twinomujuni Johnson* Criminal Session Case No. 191/98: Where a judge decides to convict in the absence of corroboration, it must be manifest in the judgment that the court has directed itself to the question of corroboration.

CASE: *Chila & Another v Republic* [1967] EA 722 East African Court of Appeal
The appellants were convicted of rape on the uncorroborated evidence of the complainant without the trial judge in his summing up or his judgement making any mention of the necessity of corroboration.

Held on appeal: The trial judge should warn the assessors and himself of the danger of acting on the uncorroborated testimony of the complainant but having done so, he may convict in the absence of corroboration if he is satisfied that her evidence is truthful. If no such warning is given, then the conviction will normally be set aside unless the appellant court is satisfied that there has been no failure of justice.

In *Katumba James v Uganda* Criminal Appeal No. 45/99, the Supreme Court of Uganda cited *Chila and Another* with approval and said:

> In the case of *Chila and Another* R [1967] EA 722 the East African Court of Appeal quashed a conviction for rape on grounds *inter alia*, that the trial judge neither warned the assessors nor himself of the desirability of corroboration. The court held that a trial judge should warn the assessors and himself of the danger of acting on the uncorroborated evidence of the complainant, but having done so he may convict in the absence of corroboration if he is satisfied that her evidence is truthful. If no such warning is given, then the conviction will normally be set aside unless the appellate court is satisfied that there has been no failure of justice. See also *Jackson Zita v Uganda* Criminal Appeal No. 19/95 Supreme Court. We respectfully agree with the above statement of the law.

Result: The court quashed the conviction for rape on grounds *inter alia* that the trial judge neither warned the assessor nor himself of the desirability of corroboration.

CASE: *Charles Katende v Uganda* [1971] HCB 313 High Court
The High Court quashed a conviction of rape because 'the complainant's story was not corroborated in material particulars and the Chief Magistrate (trial court) had not warned himself of the danger of convicting in the absence of such corroborative evidence'.

CASE: *Chiu Nang Hong v Public Prosecutor* [1964] 1 WLR1279
It was stated by the Privy Council that where in a rape trial, the trial judge had in mind the risk of convicting without corroboration, but had decided to do so because he was convinced of the truth of the complainant's evidence, he should make it clear that he had had the risk in question in mind but nevertheless was convinced by the evidence, even though uncorroborated, that the case against the accused was established beyond reasonable doubt. *No particular form is necessary for that purpose, what is necessary is that the judge's mind on the matter should be clearly revealed.* (My emphasis)

CASE: *Edmund Wladyslaw Brotow Zielinski* 1950 Court of Criminal Appeal
In a trial for indecent assault, the trial judge told the jury what was meant in law by corroboration, told them of the desirability of looking for it and warned them of the danger of convicting in its absence, but did not point out to them any piece of evidence which was capable in law of amounting to corroboration.

On appeal against conviction, the Court of Criminal Appeal held *inter alia* that: where a judge has given the jury an adequate warning on corroboration and has explained to them what is meant in law by corroboration, it is unnecessary that he should point out to the jury the piece of evidence which can amount to corroboration.

The rule on corroboration applies to all ingredients of a sexual offence

In *Uganda v Rurahukayo John* Criminal Session Case No. 260/97 High Court it was held that in a sexual offence the court must find corroboration of the complainant's testimony on all ingredients. This corroboration is required as a matter of judicial caution and practice. It may be adduced from direct and/or circumstantial evidence.

In *Mugoya Wilson v Uganda* Criminal Appeal No.8/1999 Supreme Court the court quoted with approval the case of *Kibale Ishima v Uganda* Criminal Appeal No.21/1998 in which the Supreme Court said *inter alia*:

> In sexual offence corroboration of the complainant's evidence implicating an accused person is a requirement for conviction of the accused. In the case of *Chilla and Another v Republic* [1967] EA 722 at 727 the Court of Appeal for East Africa said 'The law in East Africa on corroboration in sexual offences is as follows:

> The judge should warn the assessors and himself of the danger of acting on the uncorroborated testimony of the complainant, but having done so he may convict in the absence of corroboration if he is satisfied that her evidence is truthful. If no warning is given, then the conviction will normally be set aside unless the appellate court is satisfied that there has been no failure of justice.'

> What was said in that case is still good law.

> The nature of corroboration to which the Court was referring in the Kibale Ishima case is independent evidence implicating an accused with the offence for which he is indicted …..

> In Osborne's *Concise Dictionary* (supra) it is defined as independent evidence which implicates a person accused of a crime by connecting him with it; evidence which confirms in some material particular not only that the crime has been committed but also that the accused committed it. That form of corroboration is required, *inter alia*, in case of accomplice witnesses and in sexual offences. … some additional evidence rendering it probable that the story of the (victim) is true and that it is reasonably safe to act upon it. It must be independent evidence which affects the accused by connecting him or tending to connect him with the crime, confirming in some material particulars not only the evidence that the crime has been committed but also that the accused committed it. It is not necessary to have confirmation of all the circumstances of the crime. Corroboration of some material particular tending to implicate the accused is enough and whilst the nature of the corroboration will necessarily vary according to the particular circumstances of the offence charged it is sufficient it is merely circumstantial evidence of his connection with the crime. Corroboration may also be found in the conduct of the accused. What was said in *R v Baskerville* (1916) 2 KB 658 about corroboration of an accomplice's evidence applies equally to evidence of a complainant in a sexual offence.

> There is need for corroboration that the victim was defiled. As it was in the instant case, this can be in the form of medical evidence confirming the complainant's testimony that she was defiled.

> There must in addition, be corroboration that it was the accused who defiled the victim. A trial judge and an appellant court must warn itself of the legal requirement for corroboration implicating the appellant. Where this is not done, it would be unsafe to convict the accused.

It is possible to convict on uncorroborated evidence

In spite of the general requirement for corroboration, the court can convict an accused on the basis of uncorroborated evidence of the complainant if court is convinced about the truthfulness of the complainant.

CASE: *Ndaula John v Uganda* Criminal Appeal No. 91/99 Court of Appeal
The appellant was convicted of rape by the High Court. He appealed on the ground that he had been convicted on the uncorroborated evidence of the complainant.

The complainant testified that the appellant put his penis in her private parts. A medical examination was carried out a day after the incident but the doctor did not find any injuries in the complainant's private parts, but found injuries on multiple body parts, especially on the abdomen. The doctor also submitted that the complainant was about 55 years old and her hymen was already ruptured.

Held:

- It was a question of fact whether the complainant had been raped or not. The trial judge was entitled to base proof of sexual intercourse on the testimony of the complainant if found truthful. The complainant had had sexual intercourse previously and in that case her hymen could not have been intact. She told the people who answered her alarm that the appellant had had sexual intercourse with her. She impressed the trial judge as a truthful witness and the trial judge was entitled to believe her testimony.
- The injuries found on the complainant's body indicated that force had been used and that negatived consent.
- The appellant was very well known to the complainant and it was not disputed that the appellant was seen getting out of the complainant's house at the time the complainant alleged that he had raped her.
- The trial judge did not warn himself of the danger of convicting on uncorroborated evidence. He however warned the assessors about the point, which indicates that he was alive to that legal requirement.

Note: In the High Court holding which was upheld by the Court of Appeal in this case the judge had correctly observed: '[Counsel for the defendant] submitted that there was no rape at all as no injuries could be found in (the complainant's) private parts and the hymen had been ruptured a long time ago. In my view, no one could reasonably expect that an old woman, a widow and thus once married could still be having her hymen intact or still be a virgin!'

CASE: *Katima John v Uganda* Criminal Appeal No. 23/99 Court of Appeal for Uganda
The court stated: Where the trial judge has an opportunity of observing the complainant as she gives her evidence and believes her to be a truthful witness, the judge can convict an accused in spite of the fact that his identity was not corroborated, i.e. even where the complainant's evidence in regard to the identity of her assailant is uncorroborated, the trial judge can convict the accused if he is satisfied with the truthfulness of the complainant. In the instant case the court observed that the complainant knew the accused before the assault, the accused detained the victim for a whole night. Court believed that in the circumstances, the complainant could not

have been mistaken about the identity of the defiler. (*Chila and Another v Republic* [1967] EA 722).

CASE: *Yozefu Nyagahakwa v Uganda* Criminal Appeal No. 340/71
The court stated:

> While it was not a rule of law that an accused person charged with rape could not be convicted on the uncorroborated evidence of the prosecutrix, it had long been the custom of the Court of Appeal to look for and require corroboration in sexual cases. If the court however came to the conclusion that in the particular case the woman was speaking the truth, then the fact that there was no corroboration mattered not at all.

CASE: *Uganda v Twinoburyo Stephen and Muzaale Philip* Criminal Case No. 353/95 High Court
The judge re-stated the rule on corroboration, that in sexual offences corroboration of the complainant's evidence must be looked for. Such corroborating evidence must be other evidence which independently links and implicates the accused with the offence (*Uganda v K.K. Shah* [1966] EA30):

> The trial judge may however go ahead and convict the accused of a sexual offence in the absence of corroboration after warning the assessors and himself of the dangers of convicting on the uncorroborated evidence of the complainant if he is convinced that the complainant's evidence is truthful (*Chila v Republic* [1967] EA 722)

The possibility of convicting in the absence of corroboration was recognised even in the infamous ruling of Lord Justice Salmon in (1969) 53 Crim App Rep 150 when he said:

> The judge should convey to the jury that… in cases of alleged sexual offences it is really dangerous to convict on the evidence of the woman or girl alone. … The judge should then go on to tell the jury that, bearing that warning well in mind, they have to look at the particular facts of the particular case and if, having given full weight to the warning, they come to the conclusion that in the particular case the woman or girl without any real doubt is speaking the truth, then the fact that there is no corroboration matters not at all; they are entitled to convict.

CASE: In *Katumba James v Uganda* Criminal Appeal No. 45/99 Supreme Court the court held that it is true that a court is not prevented from convicting a person of sexual offence on the evidence of the complainant alone if she is believed by the court to be a truthful witness. But the practice in such a case consistently and rightly has been that the complainant's evidence be corroborated. It is generally considered unsafe to base a conviction only on the evidence of a complainant in sexual offences.

CASE: *Telesfora Alex & Another v R* 1963 EA 141[3]
The two appellants were convicted on charges of having committed an unnatural offence and robbery. Available medical evidence was that the complainant had been carnally assaulted. He identified the appellants as his assaulters. He testified that he had been threatened with a razor blade and was also robbed of a 5 shilling note.

When the appellants were arrested a 5 shilling note and a razor blade were found in the possession of the second appellant. There was also evidence of semen stains on the articles of clothing worn by the appellants. Both appellants admitted that at the time of their arrest they were together with the complainant and had been together with him for some time.

In convicting the appellants the magistrate failed to warn himself of the need for corroboration of the evidence of the complainant identifying the appellants as his assailants.

Issue: whether there was evidence which, had the magistrate given himself the necessary warning, would have led inevitably to the conclusion that the evidence of the complainant implicating the appellants was sufficiently corroborated.

Held on appeal:

> The irresistible inference from the medical evidence, when considered in the light of the other circumstantial evidence was that the two appellants were with the complainant at the time he was assaulted and that they had committed both offences.

> Had the magistrate directed himself as to the need for corroboration he would have undoubtedly convicted the appellants on the evidence before him.

Result: Appeals dismissed.

CASE: *Katimba v Uganda* [1967] EA 363

The appellant was charged with various counts including indecent assault (Section 122(1) of the Uganda Penal Code). He was convicted of indecent assault. The only evidence to support the charge was the uncorroborated evidence of the female herself.

On appeal it was **held** *inter alia* by the High Court that:

> The trial magistrate failed to consider the question of corroboration. Non-direction may amount to misdirection and so it is in this case. The only witness was the complainant. The learned magistrate never even mentioned the question of corroboration; nor did he say that he accepted the evidence because he found the complainant honest and truthful. As a rule of practice, on a charge of indecent assault it is not safe to convict on the uncorroborated evidence of the prosecutrix. But if the jury is satisfied of her veracity and warning themselves of the danger of such conviction, they may nevertheless convict.

Result: Appeal upheld.

Examples of corroboration

Case law reveals what is usually taken as circumstantial evidence for purposes of proving the fact of penetration, the identity of the assaulter as well as the absence of consent. The statutory questions asked in Police Form 3 and cited below also reflect preconceived ideas about rape:

1. Question 3: If the hymen is ruptured, how long ago?
2. Question 7: Are there any injuries or bruises on the thighs, legs, arms, elbows and back?
3. Question 8: Are the injuries or bruises in 7 above consistent with her putting up some form of resistance?
4. Question 9: Is the female strong and capable of putting up some form of resistance?

No hard and fast rule as to what constitutes corroboration

Although case law provide examples of what courts have taken as evidence to corroborate the complainant's story, each case must be taken on its own facts and one can state that there are no hard and fast rules as to what constitutes corroboration as was aptly stated by the Court of Appeal for Uganda below in *Kayondo Robert v Uganda* Criminal Appeal No. 18/96.

> There is no hard and fast rule as to what constitutes corroborative evidence. Each case must depend upon its own facts. Among the corroborating circumstances almost generally present in cases of rape are the signs and marks of struggle upon the complainant which strengthens her evidence of lack of consent.

> Uncorroborated evidence of the complainant would be considered insufficient to base on a conviction if it contained numerous and serious contradictions.

The presence of bruises does not always constitute corroboration

CASE: *Abasi Kibazo v Uganda* [1965] EA 507 East African Court of Appeal
Although 'medical evidence' was to the effect that 'bruises were found in the vagina of the complainant' the court stated that such bruises have been known to occur to women who have given their consent to sexual intercourse depending, of course, on the size of the male organ and the manner in which intercourse takes place.

State of victim's clothes as evidence of corroboration

In *Uganda v Lt Col Issa Habib Galungube* High Court Criminal Session Case No. 30/89 the court noted that '[The complainant's] dress was normal and smart and ... no injuries were found upon her particularly in her private parts'. Court did not therefore believe that the accused's sexual intercourse with the complainant was non-consensual. Court was doubtful about the complainant's claim that she did not consent or that she was not a girlfriend of the accused.

In *Safari Innocent v Uganda* Criminal Appeal No. 20/1995 Supreme Court, the condition of the victim's clothes, i.e torn knickers, was taken as corroboration of the victim's story.

Corroboration of absence of consent/Corroboration of identity of accused

CASE: *Lawi Ongweya v Republic* [1964] EA 129 High Court of Tanganyika.
The appellant was charged with rape. The complainant's story was that while she was walking on the road she was set upon by the appellant and that he had sexual intercourse with her several times. At first she struggled, but when he threatened her with a knife she ceased to resist. She immediately complained of the rape to more than one person, giving a description of the appellant's outward appearance and clothing. There was medical evidence of bruising on her thighs and legs. When she complained to her sister, she was trembling and had grass in her hair. The complainant also told a detective that the assaulter had a scar on the inner side of his left thigh. After the arrest of the appellant he was identified as the man who had assaulted her. A scar as had been described by the complainant was also found on his body.

The magistrate held that he could find no corroboration in the strict sense of the word of the complainant's story as implicating the appellant and then having warned himself of the danger of convicting on the uncorroborated evidence of the complainant convicted the appellant on the ground that he was convinced of the truthfulness of her story.

On appeal it was **held**:

1. The fact that the complainant correctly described the appellant's outward appearance and clothing was no corroboration of her evidence that he was her assailant. But her knowledge that he had a scar on the inside of his left thigh was a circumstance corroborative of her assertion that it was he who had sexually assaulted her. It was wholly incompatible with the assertion of the appellant, who was an admitted stranger to her, that 'he knew nothing about her'.

2. There was thus corroboration of the complainant's story not only that her assailant had intercourse with her against her will, but also that her assailant was the appellant.

In his judgement the appellate judge also stated that the fact that the complainant made an early report and was trembling when she made a report to her sister was sufficient corroboration that whoever had intercourse with her had done so without her consent.

The appellate judge also stated that:

> Strictly speaking, the fact that the complainant described the appellant's outward appearance and clothing correctly cannot be held to corroborate her evidence that he was her assailant. For she might, for some unknown reason, have seen the appellant innocently walking in her vicinity and decided falsely to incriminate him by giving a description of his personal appearance and clothing and saying that a man of that description had raped her. And she could have done this after no more than a casual glance at him. But there was one peculiarity by which she described him which afforded true circumstantial corroboration of her allegations against him – the scar on the inside of his left thigh – a mark she could not have seen unless he had been very close to her without his trousers on.

Result: Appeal dismissed.

CASE: *Uganda v Abel Ochan* [1972] (1) ULR 13 High Court

The accused was charged with rape. After the alleged incident the complainant immediately reported to her stepson and later to the chief. The accused was found lying completely naked inside the house within a short time. The trousers which the complainant picked up and carried away belonged to the accused. The complainant's necklace was broken and the beads were found scattered on the floor inside the hut where the accused was lying. The injuries sustained by the complainant showed that force had been used against her.

Held: Circumstantial evidence implicating the accused could be corroboration. On the facts as established there was ample corroboration of the complainant's evidence.

Failure to make a prompt report not necessarily fatal to prosecution case

CASE: *Eria Ngobi v R* (1953) 20 EACA 154 Court of Appeal for Eastern Africa

The appellant was charged with the rape of a girl aged about 7 years. The girl had made no complaint to any of her family but her mother noticed her inability to walk properly. There was evidence that she had been with the appellant the day she was assaulted. Three days later she was found to be suffering from a new infection of gonorrhoea and the appellant was found to be suffering from an old infection of the same complaint. The appellant was convicted of indecent assault but he appealed on the ground that there was not sufficient evidence in corroboration of the girl's story. It was pointed out that she had not made a prompt report and might well never have spoken of it at all but for the fact that her mother noticed her inability to walk properly.

Held *inter alia*: There were sufficient pointers to justify a finding that the evidence given by the girl which implicated the appellant was substantially true. First there was evidence that the girl had been in the company of the appellant on the day she was assaulted. She was found with a new infection of gonorrhoea and when the appellant was examined, he was suffering from an old infection of the same complaint.

CASE: In *Chila & Another v Republic* [1967] EA 722 it was **held** *inter alia* that subsequent complainant by an alleged victim to a third party does not in itself constitute corroboration since it may be due to remorse, or to fear of the consequences of sexual intercourse, or some other reason.

Distressed condition of the complainant can amount to corroboration
In several cases courts have held the distressed condition of the complainant in a sexual offence to amount to corroboration of the complainant's evidence.

In *R v Alan Redpath* (1962), 46 Crim App Rep 319 the Lord Chief Justice stated as follows:

> It seems that the distressed condition of a complainant is quite clearly capable of amounting to corroboration. Of course, the circumstances will vary enormously, and in some circumstances quite clearly no weight, or little weight, could be attached to such evidence as corroboration. Thus, if a girl goes in a distressed condition to her mother and makes a complaint, while the mother's evidence as to the girl's condition may in law be capable of amounting to corroboration, quite clearly the jury should be told that they should attach little, if any weight to that evidence, because it is all part and parcel of the complaint. The girl making the complaint might well put on an act and simulate distress.

See also *Lawi Ongweya v Republic* [1964] EA129 High Court of Tanganyika where among other things the distressed condition of the complainant when she reported to her sister immediately after the assault, was taken as corroboration that the sexual intercourse had been non-consensual.

In *Nsubuga Daniel v Uganda, Criminal Appeal No. 69/1997* the judge said:

> It is trite law that the distressed condition of the complainant acts as sufficient corroboration to the act of sexual intercourse. (*see Sekabazo v Uganda* 1965 EA 507)

In *Uganda v Kakooza Sulaiman* Criminal Session Case No.0072/99 the Court held that the distressed condition of the complainant when she reported the defilement to her father was corroboration of her testimony.

In *Kintu Charles v. Uganda* Criminal Appeal No. 68/97 Court of Appeal/ Supreme Court it was **held** *inter alia* that:

In sexual offences the court should warn itself of the danger of acting on uncorroborated evidence of the complainant but having done so it may convict in the absence of corroboration if it is satisfied that the complainants' evidence is truthful. (See *Boona Peter v Uganda* Criminal Appeal No. 16/1997, Court of Appeal for Uganda). In the instant case the court held that the evidence of the complainant's mother regarding the condition she was in when she reported to her shortly after the defilement supplies the corroboration, if one was required.

On appeal to the Supreme Court, the Supreme Court *inter alia* held that the complainant's testimony was amply corroborated by her mothers' evidence that the complainant was in a distressed condition when she first reported to her mother.

In *Kato Sula v Uganda* Criminal Appeal No. 30/99 Court of Appeal the complainant's grandfather observed the victim's distressed condition and testified on the matter. It was held that a distressed condition of a victim in appropriate cases may serve as corroboration of her evidence. Cited *Abasi Kibazo v Uganda* with approval.

CASE: *Safari Innocent v Uganda* Criminal Appeal No. 20/95 Supreme Court
The accused (appellant) and the victim were neighbours and knew each other. The accused forcefully had sexual intercourse with the victim. The victim reported the incident to her parents the same evening, naming the accused as the culprit. The accused could not be traced that evening. On the following morning, he turned up at the victim's home and begged for mercy. The victim's father reported the incident to the police and the appellant was arrested on the same evening of the assault. The victim was taken for medical examination and the doctor estimated her age to be between 13 and 14. Medical evidence also revealed that the victim's vagina had a raw area and was congested with blood. The hymen was torn. There was fresh discharge from the vagina.

The appellant was convicted of defilement of a girl under 18 years.

He appealed against conviction on the following grounds:
1. The prosecution failed to prove that the complainant was under 18 years.
2. It was not shown that it was the appellant who defiled the complainant.

Several facts were taken as corroboration. The Supreme Court held *inter alia* that the evidence of the complainant that she had been defiled was clearly corroborated by the medical evidence, the fact of her torn knickers, her distressed condition, the medical evidence that her hymen was torn. That it was the appellant who had defiled her was clear from the appellant's subsequent confession to, and request for mercy from the complainant's mother.

Medical evidence as corroboration

Medical evidence can be used to corroborate the allegation that the complainant had sexual intercourse, that the intercourse was without her consent and that it was the accused person who had intercourse with the complainant.

CASE: *Karim Zawedde Abdu v Uganda* Criminal Appeal No. 14/98
The appellant was convicted of defilement of a girl under 18 years of age and was convicted. One of the grounds of appeal submitted by counsel for the appellant was that the trial judge erred to find that the doctor's finding of the existence of pus in the

complainant's private parts and in the urethra of the appellant was corroboration of the fact that it was the appellant who had defiled the complainant. He contended that this was a wrong conclusion because the pus from both the complainant and the appellant was not cultured to determine the nature of the organisms.

In response the learned Principal State Attorney for the respondent submitted that failure to culture the pus from the appellant and the complainant was not fatal to the case. The pus found in the complainant's private parts and in the appellant's urethra was one piece of circumstantial evidence which the trial judge relied on. In his judgement the learned trial judge found that the complainant was a truthful witness and warned himself of the danger of convicting on the uncorroborated evidence of the complainant. Counsel submitted further that there was other corroborative evidence on record which the trial judge took into account. This was that the appellant ran away when the local authorities went to arrest him, which conduct was inconsistent with the innocence of the appellant.

Court of Appeal **held** that:

> We entirely agree with the submissions of the State Attorney. The learned trial judge found the complainant truthful and further more there was corroboration of her evidence in the doctor's report, the evidence of her grandmother (PW6) and the evidence of PW3 who went to arrest the appellant and he ran away.

Desirable that medical evidence is provided by qualified medical practitioner

CASE: *Abasi Kibazo v Uganda* [1965] EA 507 East African Court of Appeal
The prosecution relied on the evidence of a medical assistant who stated that he had found bruises in the complainant's vagina. The trial court accepted the opinion of this witness that in view of the bruises found on the complainant, the intercourse with her took place by force and without her consent. On appeal the Court of Appeal **held** *inter alia* that the medical assistant, who was not a qualified doctor, should not have been allowed to express an opinion without laying down a foundation of sufficient experience enabling him to speak with authority on the subject. It was highly desirable that such evidence as he gave should come from a qualified medical practitioner.
Result: Acquittal.

Conduct of the accused may constitute corroboration

In *Katumba James v Uganda* Criminal Appeal No. 45/99 Supreme Court, the flight of the accused from the scene of the alleged crime when people who answered the complainant's alarm arrived constituted corroboration of the complainant's testimony that the accused had had sexual intercourse with her without her consent.

CASE: *Safari Innocent v Uganda* Criminal Appeal No. 20/95 Supreme Court
The accused (appellant) and the victim were neighbours and knew each other. The accused forcefully had sexual intercourse with the victim. He was convicted of defilement but appealed *inter alia* on the ground that it was not shown that it was the appellant who defiled the complainant.

The Supreme Court **held** *inter alia* that: The prosecution evidence that the appellant disappeared from his home in the neighbourhood and could not be traced at the material time and his confession and plea for mercy also clearly supported the complainant's evidence that it was the appellant who sexually assaulted her that evening.

Conduct of accused can corroborate complainant's testimony as to identity of assaulter

CASE: *Uganda v Rashid Busasi* Criminal Session Case No. 419/95 High Court
Where the court considers the conduct of an accused to be inconsistent with innocence, such conduct can act as corroboration of the testimony of the victim in regard to identification of the accused.

Disappearance of accused from his home can offer corroboration of his guilt

CASE: *Remigious Kiwanuka v Uganda* Criminal Appeal No. 41/95 Supreme Court
The appellant was convicted of defilement. The only issue on appeal was whether it was the appellant who defiled the complainant. The fact that she had been defiled and that she was under the age of 18 years were conceded by the appellant's counsel, as having been proved by the prosecution to the required standard.
The Supreme Court **held** *inter alia* that:

> It is settled law that in sexual offences though corroboration of the prosecution evidence is not essential in law, it is, in practice always looked for, and it is the established practice to warn the assessors against the danger of acting upon uncorroborated testimony. This rule of practice applies with the same force even in a case where there is no dispute that a sexual offence has been committed and the question is one of identity only. See Archbold *Criminal Evidence and Practice*, 39th ed. para 2887.

The Supreme Court cited *Chila and Another v Republic* [1967] EA 722 with approval and held that 'the disappearance of an accused person from the area of a crime soon after the incident may provide corroboration to other evidence that he has committed the offence. This is because such sudden disappearance from the area is incompatible with innocent conduct of such a person.' In this case corroboration could be found in the appellant's disappearance from his house and the school compound soon after the incident.
Result: Appeal dismissed.

CASE: *Kato Sula v Uganda* Criminal Appeal No. 30/1999 Court of Appeal
The accused was convicted of defiling a pupil in the school where he was a teacher. The only eyewitness to the sexual intercourse was the victim. On corroboration of identification, the Court of Appeal held that the disappearance of the accused (appellant) from his place of abode after the incident corroborated the complainant's statement that it was the appellant who defiled her.

Corroboration of sexual offences when combined with other offences

Is corroboration required in a sexual offence where the accused allegedly committed not only a sexual offence but other offences as well in the same event?

In answering the above question, the Supreme Court of Jamaica in *Regina v Derrick Williams* clearly brought out the shaky ground on which the rule on corroboration stands.

CASE: *Regina v Derrick Williams* Jamaica Supreme Court Criminal Appeal No.12/98 The appellant was convicted of illegal possession of firearms and of rape. The brief facts were that he approached the complainant with a gun and demanded that she shut up. He hit her with a gun in the face causing a wound and thereafter raped her. At his trial he denied owning a gun and also said he had never seen the complainant until the day of trial. He appealed against the conviction on the ground that the learned trial judge did not express that there was no evidence of corroboration and that being so that he had warned himself of the danger of acting on the uncorroborated evidence of the complainant before accepting her as a witness of truth.

Speaking of circumstances where the sexual offence is just one of several offences charged, e.g. burglary or robbery the court said:

> ... the absurdity of calling for a special warning on corroboration for the sexual offence when the only issue is identity. In those circumstances, if one applies the corroboration rules strictly, the woman's evidence about the identity of the intruder requires no corroboration if he confines himself to robbing or stealing, but must be the subject of the usual warning if, having stolen or robbed, he then goes on to rape the woman, despite the fact that the rape would almost certainly give her more opportunity and more incentive to observe and memorise his appearance than the robbery or theft. If the law demands that in those or similar circumstances the usual warning should be given by the judge, it puts an unexpected and unwelcome premium on rape. Presumably also in such circumstances, the judge would have the task of explaining to the jury that it would be dangerous to convict on the uncorroborated evidence of the victim in respect of the rape but not dangerous so far as the robbery was concerned. Moreover, any judge might be forgiven for hesitating long before adding insult to injury by explaining to a jury the reasons for the usual warning, namely that the unfortunate householder, allegedly burgled and raped in her own home, might have made a false accusation owing to sexual neurosis, fantasy, spite or refusal to admit consent of which she is now ashamed or any of the other reasons in *R v Manning*.

Justification for the rule on corroboration

The alledged justification for the requirement of 'corroboration' in cases involving sexual offences has its origins in the opinion of Sir Mathew Hale (Kings Bench England) in 1671 when he said that rape must be examined with greater caution than any other crime as it is easy to charge and difficult to defend.

Similar opinion has been expressed by Lord Justice Salmon in *R v Henry & Manning* (1969) 53 Crim App Rep 150, 153:

> What the judge has to do is to use clear and simple language that will without any doubt convey to the jury that in cases of alleged sexual offences it is really dangerous to convict on the evidence of the woman or girl alone. This is dangerous because human experience has shown that in these cases girls and women do sometimes tell an entirely false story which is very easy to fabricate, but extremely difficult to refute. Such stories are fabricated for all sorts of reasons, which I need not enumerate, and sometimes for no reason at all.

The reasons historically given for such fabrications are that women are by nature peculiarly prone to malice and mendacity, and particularly adept at concealing it. It is said that a woman may be motivated by fantasy, sexual neurosis, spite, jealousy, revenge, psychological or physiological problems, embarrassment in front of a spouse or partner or simple refusal to admit consent to an act which she later regretted. At the beginning of the twentieth century Sigmund Freud came up with some theories to explain women's behaviour. He defined women as 'castrated men' and as having a 'lack', since they do not possess the male sex organ (Juliet Mitchell and Rose (eds) *Female Sexuality*). It was contended that due to penis envy women are pushed into fabricating false accusations against men.

In its Consultation Paper on the Law of Rape, the Law Reform Commission of Ireland[4] quotes yet another bizarre prejudice against women in favour of the corroboration requirement:

> A number of different motives may prompt a deliberately falsified accusation of rape. A woman may consent to sexual intercourse with a man, then feel ashamed of herself and bitter at her partner, and bring charges of rape against him. Or she may have become pregnant and accuse an entirely innocent party for the purpose of shielding the man who actually caused her pregnancy. A woman may falsify charges for the purpose of blackmail. Or she may do so solely out of hatred or revenge, or for notoriety.

This stereotyping of women has found its way into criminal law text books. For example, Glanville Williams, an English authority on criminal law states that a woman's consent to sex is a 'hazy concept', their intentions are vacillating, ill-defined and unreliable and women have 'obscure psychological reasons' for behaving the way they do.[5]

These sexist allegations about women can only be propounded by 'theorists' and jurists who are devoid of any insight into the impact of rape on a woman in a patriarchal society. In a society where the *fact* of a woman having had numerous sexual partners devalues and demeans her; a society where rape is culturally seen as sordid; a society which stigmatises the victim of rape, how likely is it that a woman would falsify a rape accusation 'solely for notoriety' or 'spite', or 'for no reason at all'?

Given the nature of the offence, corroboration may not be easy to find. It is unlikely that a rapist will commit the offence in the presence of witnesses. The victim may be too traumatised to report the assault immediately after it has occurred. She may also not be in a position to collect and preserve evidence and exhibits that could be used in the event of prosecution. The majority of victims do not have access to medical personnel who could examine them immediately after the ordeal and preserve the necessary evidence such as the body fluids of the suspect found in the body of the victim. The requirement of corroboration is thus often incongruous with effective prosecution.

Some analysts who support the rule on corroboration argue that it is a rule applicable to all sexual offences and therefore not specific to women. It is, however, a statistical fact that the majority of victims of sexual assaults are women and thus, since the rule disproportionately affects women, it can be challenged as a form of gender discrimination. It has the effect of impairing the right of a woman to the protection of the law. Where the effect of a requirement has an adverse impact disproportionately on one group of people, this is recognised as indirect discrimination. The rule on corroboration is thus unconstitutional for being discriminatory against women.

Aware that for most other crimes, the word of the victim is sufficient evidence to sustain a conviction, why is the word of a victim not taken in a sexual assault? And just as it is in other criminal prosecutions, an accused can only be convicted of rape if the prosecution proves its case against him beyond reasonable doubt, is this not enough protection against false accusations?

And as already pointed out, supporters of the requirement for corroboration justify their support on the basis that women have a tendency to make false accusations of rape. Even if it were true, one can argue that the false accusations can be made in other crimes and therefore the question is: why is there no corroboration requirement in such other offences? Is cross examination not sufficient as it is with other crimes to detect falsehood?

A critical analysis of court pronouncements in rape trials often leads to the conclusion that as pointed out by Bruce A. MacFarlane, whereas statutory law may appear as intended to protect women against unwanted sexual advances, courts often appear to bend over backwards to acquit in all but the most egregious situations.

It is to be noted that no particular words are necessary for the purpose of the warning on conviction without corroboration. What is necessary is that the judge's mind should be alive to the danger. It is further noted that the need for corroboration is applicable to all the ingredients of the particular offence. Thus in rape, there is need to corroborate the fact of sexual intercourse, the identity of the assaulter and the absence of consent.

A discussion of the rape trial, especially in regard to the rule on corroboration leads to the conclusion that the prosecution of sexual offences is unlike the prosecution of other criminal offences. There is a preoccupation with aspects of the complainant's behaviour and life history which may not be immediately related to the alleged assault. Thus, the prosecution may lose its case on the basis of what would appear irrelevant facts in other cases, e.g if the victim takes a long time before reporting the assault; if the prosecution does not prove that the victim appeared very distraught at the time she reported the assault; or if the defence proves that the victim is a prostitute. Rules which shift the usual focus of a criminal trial from an inquiry into the conduct of the accused to that of the moral worth of the complainant give legitimacy to the saying that rape is the only offence wherein the victim is treated as an offender.

There is evidence that judges in Uganda have started questioning the desirability of the rule on corroboration. For example in *Uganda v Peter Matovu* Criminal Session Case no. 146/2001 Justice E.S. Lugayizi did not hesitate to condemn the rule as unconstitutional. His Lordship bodly stated that court would not apply the said rule "because it discriminates against women and is, therefore in conflict with Uganda's international obligations and the constitution". Although the case was in the High Court and not in the Supreme Court, Lugayizi's pronouncements offer hope to categories of people who have hitherto been denied justice as a result of the rule. Below are the facts and relevant ruling in *Uganda v Peter Matovu*.

Facts and Ruling

The accused was indicted for defilement of a girl under the age of 18 years. In reference to the rule on corroboration Justice Lugayizi pointed out that the rule is one of practice. His Lordship drew attention to the alleged justification of the rule thus: "to safeguard men against unwanted prosecutions or false accusations in respect of sexual offences courts have always insisted upon the above rule of practice before convictions can be had". He then went on to say;

> Be that as it may, Court has not come across any empirical data or basis for the belief that women are greater liars than men or, for that matter that they are much more likely to lie than to say the truth in matters concerning sexual allegations. For that reason it seems that both the belief and the resultant rule have no logical basis. Therefore, the question Court wishes to raise here, is whether the said rule is legally justifiable? Court proposes to answer that question in the negative. It will base its stand on the premises below.

> Firstly, Court is of the opinion that the said rule is in conflict with section 132 of the Evidence Act (Cap.43) which provides as follows,

> 'Subject to the provisions of any other law in force, no particular number of witnesses shall in any case be required for the proof of any fact.'

> In essence, the above provision lays down a general rule and an exception. In simple terms, the general rule is that the evidence of one witness is enough to prove any fact in any case. The exception to the rule is that where "any other law in force" provides so, the evidence of more than one witness may be required, in any case, to prove any fact. In Court's opinion the exception to the general rule in section 132 of the Evidence Act only covers 'any other law in force' which is the creature of the legislature; and certainly it does not cover a mere rule of practice that courts may wish to observe. To interpret the exception differently would bring into the picture all kinds of possibilities. For example, that even unwritten customary law, etc. may, legally, furnish an exception to the general rule in section 132 of the Evidence Act. Court greatly doubts whether that was the intention of the legislature. From that standpoint alone, Court is of the opinion that the said rule is not legally justifiable, for it cannot stand as a valid exception to the general rule in section 132 of the Evidence Act.

> Secondly, and much more importantly, Court thinks that the above rule discriminates against women who, are, by far, the most frequent victims of sexual offences and is, therefore, inconsistent with Uganda's international obligations under various conventions and the Constitution.

> The *Collins English Dictionary and Thesaurus* defines the word 'discrimination' as follows,

> *The singling out of a particular person, group, etc. for special favour or disfavour.*

> The Convention on the Elimination of all forms of Discrimination Against Women (1979) (Also known as CEDAW) provides a more elaborate definition of the word 'discrimination' when applied in relation to women. Article 1 CEDAW provides as follows,

> *'discrimination against women' shall mean any distinction, exclusion or restriction made on the basis of sex which has the effect or purpose of impairing or nullifying the recognition, enjoyment or exercise by women irrespective of their marital status, on a basis of equality of men and women of human rights and fundamental freedoms in the*

political, economic, cultural, civil or any other field.

The rule easily falls within the four walls of the above definitions. For, clearly, its effect is to single out women for disfavour in cases involving sexual allegations in the sense that it nullifies the recognition, enjoyment or exercise of their rights to equality before the law and equal protection of the law. Indeed, in such cases, the testimony of a victim is not, of itself, valuable. It is suspect; and this is, essentially, because she is a woman or a girl! (See Neville and 3 others – supra). Uganda ratified CEDAW and the various conventions, which constitute the International Bill of Rights. In addition, under Article 21 of the Constitution that proclaims equality of all persons under the law, equal protection of the law and prohibition against discrimination on the ground of sex, Uganda enacted the heart of the above international instruments in one stroke. Therefore, Uganda has the obligation to give effect to the contents of those international instruments. For that reason, the above rule that discriminates against women and is inconsistent with Uganda's international obligations and the Constitution is not legally justifiable. Under Article 2 of the Constitution the fate of any law that is inconsistent with the Constitution is very clear. Such law is null and void. It follows, therefore, that the above rule is null and void.

In concluding this area of the judgment, Court simply wishes to say that it will not apply the above rule because it discriminates against women and is, therefore, in conflict with Uganda's international obligations and the constitution.

It is hoped that courts higher in hierarchy will follow Lugayizi's analysis of the rule and refrain from applying it.

1.The rule is applicable to all sexual offences and not just rape.
2.The rule has been abolished in several jurisdictions. In England the Criminal Justice and Public Order Act (1994) which redefined sexual intercourse in rape as including both vaginal and anal penetration abolished the 'corroboration rule' which required trial judges to warn the jury of the dangers of convicting the accused solely on the evidence of a woman who complains of a sexual assault
3. Although the case is one of unnatural offences the principles enunciated is applicable to rape and indeed other sexual offences.
4. October 1987; http://www.lawreform.ie/publications/data/volume6/lrc-42.html. Accessed on 15-06-2004. Pg 116 of 171.
5. Glanville Williams (1983, 2nd Edition), *Textbook of Criminal Law.*

6

Defilement of girls under 18 years: Section 129[1] of the Uganda Penal Code Act

Section 129 provides that:

> Any person who unlawfully has sexual intercourse with a girl under the age of 18 years is guilty of an offence and is liable to suffer death.

It is this offence that is referred to as defilement of a girl under the age of 18 years. In some jurisdictions, defilement is referred to as statutory rape.

Changes by the 1990 amendment
- In 1990 the age of minimum consent to sex was raised from 14 years to 18 years.
- The maximum punishment was raised from life imprisonment to the death sentence.[2]
- The defence of reasonable belief that a girl was of minumum age was abolished.[3] Defilement is thus a 'strict liability' offence and Section 144 of the Code is applicable to the offence:

Section 144:

> Except as otherwise expressly stated, it is immaterial in the case of any offence committed with respect to a woman or girl under a specified age, that the accused person did not know that the woman or girl was under that age or believed that she was not under age.

It is noted that defilement shares several ingredients with rape and thus my discussion of defilement will be limited to a discussion of elements of defilement which are not present in rape. Principles on the ingredients common to both offences – sexual intercourse/carnal knowledge/penetration as well as the rule on corroboration – enunciated in the case law on rape are as applicable to defilement as they are to rape and will not be repeated in the discussion to follow.

Ingredients of defilement
The essential ingredients for a successful prosecution for defilement have been defined by various court rulings.

In *Agaya Robert v Uganda* Criminal Appeal No. 18/2000 Court of Appeal stated that:

> It is well settled that in order to constitute the offence of defilement, the following must be proved:
> - Sexual intercourse
> - Victim's age below 18 years
> - The accused is the culprit

In *Bassita Hussein v Uganda* Crim Appeal 35/1995 the Supreme Court also laid down the ingredients of the offence of defilement which the prosecution must prove beyond reasonable doubt as:

- The fact of sexual intercourse.
- The age of the girl victim being under 18 years.
- Participation by the accused in the alleged sexual intercourse.

Aiding defilement

As with the offence of rape, persons who aid someone who is actually committing the offence – having unlawful sexual intercourse with a girl under the age of 18 years – can be found guilty with the perpetrator. This is a consequence of Section 19 of the Uganda Penal Code which deals with principal offenders.

Section 19 Principal Offenders 19 (1)

When an offence is committed, each of the following persons is deemed to have taken part in committing the offence and to be guilty of the offence and may be charged with actually committing it.

a) every person who actually does the act or makes the omission which constitutes the offence

b) every person who does or omits to do any act for the purpose of enabling or aiding another person to commit the offence

c) every person who aids or abets another person in comitting the offence

CASE: *Kayondo, Fred and Mutagayika Silas v Uganda* Criminal Appeal No. 31/1998 The two appellants were convicted of defilement C/S 123(1) of the Penal Code. Kayondo Fred, the first appellant had sexual intercourse with the complainant while the second appellant held the complainant's hands.

Held:

Kayondo (A1) was a principal and A2 an aider and abettor. A2 assisted A1. A2 consciously participated in what was happening. He assisted A1 in ensuring that the complainant did not resist A1's sexual act. The intention of A2 in holding the hands of the complainant while A1 ravished her was to enable A1 to succeed in his act of defilement. The provisions of Section 21(1) (b) and (c) Penal Code Act[4] apply to A2.

Thus court found that the prosecution proved beyond reasonable doubt that it was A1 who had sexual intercourse with the complainant while A2 aided and abetted the defilement. Both were guilty of defilement under Section 123 of the Uganda Penal Code Act. Both were sentenced to 7 years imprisonment.

The High Court finding and sentence were confirmed by the Court of Appeal.

CASE: *Uganda v Mugoya Wilson* Criminal Session Case No. 170/93 High Court[5]
The accused was charged with defilement of two girls under the age of 18 years. He pleaded not guilty to both counts.

Held *inter alia* on the matter of the burden of proof :

It is the law that an accused should never be called upon to prove his innocence. *Woolmington v DPP* [1935]AC 462; *Oketh Okale v R* [1965] EA 555.

It is also trite law that an accused person should be convicted on the strength of the case as established by the prosecution but not on the weaknesses of his defence: *R v Israili Epuku s/o Achietu* (1934) 1 EACA 166.

Corroboration is needed on all the ingredients of the offence

As with cases of rape, for a successful prosecution of defilement, all the ingredients of the offence must be corroborated – the evidence of the victim is not in itself sufficient proof.

In *Uganda v Rurahukayo John* Criminal Session Case No. 260/97 the High Court **held** that in a sexual offence the Court must find corroboration of the complainant's testimony on all ingredients. This corroboration is required as a matter of judicial caution and practice. It may be adduced from direct and or circumstantial evidence.

The difference between rape and defilement

Defilement can be disguished from rape in three ways:

1. Marriage is not a defence
2. The age of the complainant is relevant
3. Consent of the girl is not a defence

Marriage is not a defence

Uganda recognises different types of marriages. Under the Customary Marriages (Registration) Act[6] the law recognises marriages contracted according to the customary practices of the parties. The law thereunder sets the minimum age of marriage for girls at 14 and for boys at 16 years.

Under the Marriage and Divorce of Mohammedans Act[7] the law recognises marriages consecrated according to Islamic law. Under Islamic law a girl can marry as soon as she starts her menstruation. It follos that a girl who starts menstruation before the age of majority (18 years) can marry under Islamic law.

If marriage of a girl under the age of 18 years is a valid marriage, then the husband of such a girl would not be convicted of defilement for a man cannot defile his own wife. However, since the promulgation of the 1995 Constitution a man cannot contract a valid marriage with a person under the age of 18 years. Since such a marriage would be unconstitutional and thus illegal, sexual intercourse with a girl under the age of 18 years can never be legal.

Article 31 (1) of the 1995 Constitution states:

> Men and women of the age of 18 years and above, have the right to marry and to found a family and are entitled to equal rights in marriage, during marriage and at its dissolution.

Defining 'Unlawfulness' in defilement

The word 'unlawful' appears in the definition of defilement in Section 129 of the Uganda Penal Code, as it does in Section 123, which defines the offence of rape.

CASE: *Uganda v Karim Zawedde* Criminal Session Case No. 551/96 High Court
The judge pointed out the ingredients of defilement as:

- The complainant is a girl of below 18 years at the time of the offence.
- That the complainant had sexual intercourse at the material time.

- That the said sexual intercourse was unlawful; and
- That the accused was responsible for the offence.

In regard to unlawfulness, his Lordship said:

> I am of the view that once the first two ingredients above have been properly proved, it follows that the sexual intercourse was unlawfully had; ... I wish to point out that I do not subscribe to the view, which was of course not propounded in this case but I have heard before (see *Uganda v Obbo Silver Toroto* Criminal Session Case No. 22/94).

> In that case it was suggested by counsel for the accused that the word 'unlawfully' which appears in S.123(1) PCA was purposely placed in that section by the Legislature to protect Muslims who have married girls under the age of 18 years. In my view s. 123(1) of the Penal Code Act applies to all persons, regardless of their religion, tribe, etc. and that interpretation is consistent with the provisions of Article 21 of the 1995 Constitution. If the legislature had intended that the said section would protect a certain class of people, it would have said so in no uncertain terms. In short, therefore in my opinion the word 'unlawful' appearing in S.123(1) PCA is surplusage.

In *Karim Zawedde Abdu v Uganda* Criminal Appeal No. 14/1998, the accused appealed against the conviction and sentence. One of the points appealed against was the High Court's decision that the word 'unlawful' is surplusage. In answer, the Court of Appeal agreed with the High Court that the word 'unlawful' in the section on defilement was surplusage. The court said:

> The complaint was on the interpretation of the world 'unlawful' in Section 123(1) PCP.

> The word 'unlawfully' in Section 123 (1) is not surplusage as was asserted by the learned Judge and proof of it was a legal requirement which was not discharged.

The Court of Appeal said *inter alia*:

> *Ground 3*
> The complaint was on the interpretation of the word 'unlawful' in Section 123(1) PCA. Counsel submitted that sometimes defilement may not be unlawful as the offender might be affected by evil spirits or witchcraft and has no *mens rea*.

Held that: If an offender is possessed by devils or is acting under the influence of witchcraft and such offender is believed by the trial court, such could amount to a defence of insanity according to S.12 of the PCA. However the *actus reus* of defilement contrary to section 123 (1) remains an unlawful act. Once a person has had sexual intercourse with a girl under the age of 18 years, the act is *per se* unlawful.

Issues concerning the age of the complainant

The essence of the law on defilement is the need to protect young girls from early sexual activity. Proof that the girl is under the age of 18 years is thus essential for a conviction of defilement.

Lack of knowledge of victim's age no defence

Before the 1990 amendment to the law proof by an accused person that he reasonably believed the girl to be above the prescribed age was a complete defence to a charge of defilement of an underage person. Since the 1990 amendment, this is no longer a defence.

CASE: *Tumuhairwe Vincent v Uganda* Criminal Appeal No. 29/97 Court of Appeal
The Court of Appeal **held** *inter alia* that the fact that an accused did not know that the victim in a defilement case was under 18 years of age is no defence.

Proof of age of victim

There is no need to prove the exact age of a victim. In *Uganda v Lwasa Sempijja* Criminal Session Case No. 381/96 it was **held**: In defilement the prosecution need not prove the exact age of the victim rather it must be proved that the girl was at the time of intercourse *under* the age of 18 years.

CASE: *Safari Innocent v. Uganda* Criminal Appeal No.2/95 Supreme Court
The appellant was convicted of defilement of a girl under 18 years. The victim was taken for medical examination and the doctor estimated her age to be between 13 and 14 years. The accused appealed against conviction on the following grounds:

- The prosecution failed to prove that the complainant was under 18 years.
- It was not shown that it was the appellant who defiled the complainant.

The Supreme Court **held** *inter alia* that:

> the complainant's own evidence, the evidence of her father and the medical evidence left no doubt that she was under the age of 18 at the material time. The estimate by the doctor was that the complainant appeared to be 13 and 14 years did not weaken the prosecution evidence in that regard. Her father's evidence was that she was 15 years when she was defiled must be correct ... even if she was 13 or 14 as the doctor estimated, she was still under 18 years old nonetheless and, therefore, under 18 for purposes of the offence of defilement under Section 123 (1).

Conclusion: In a charge of defilement the prosecution's duty is to prove that the victim was less than 18 years at the time of sexual intercourse. It need not prove the exact age of the victim.

CASE: *Katima John v Uganda* Criminal Appeal No. 23/99. Court of Appeal for Uganda
Katima was convicted of defilement under Section 123(1) of the Uganda Penal Code. The prosecution case was that the defilement occurred on 15 December 1992. In her evidence the complainant stated that she was told by her father that she was born in 1977 (and was therefore 15 years at the time of the assault). On the other hand, her mother testified that the girl was born in 1979 (and was therefore 13 years at the relevant time). The doctor who examined the victim determined that she was 14 years. He stated in cross examination that he did not have the machine to examine her age but used his experience.

On appeal it was argued that there was no evidence to prove that the complainant was below the age of 18 years.
Held by the Court of Appeal:

> The prosecution had proved beyond reasonable doubt that the victim was under 18 years of age. The learned judge came to the right conclusion that the complainant was

under 18 years. Even if the court believed that the complainant was born either in 1979 or 1977, she was defiled in 1995 and whichever date is taken she was definitely below 18 years. The learned trial judge observed the complainant while she was giving evidence in court, and formed his opinion about her age, which he was entitled to do.

Conclusion: In a defilement case, the prosecution need not prove the exact age of the victim. All that is needed is to prove (beyond reasonable doubt) that the victim was under the age of 18 years.

Absence of a birth certificate is not fatal to prosecution case on an indictment for defilement.

In *Uganda v Mukasa Everisto* Criminal Session Case No. 22/98 the High Court held:

> In the absence of a birth certificate the age of a person can be proved by any other lawful evidence such as testimony of a close relative. It could also be established by observation and common sense. See *GRIMSLY ex parte Purser* [1951] 2 All ER 889.

Silence by the examining doctor as to the age of the victim not fatal to prosecution case

CASE: *Uganda v Kintu Charles* Criminal Session Case No. 467/95 High Court
The accused was indicted for defiling his student.

The complainant testified that she was 14 years at time of the sexual assault. The complainant's mother testified that her daughter was 14 years at the relevant date. Although the complainant was examined by a medical doctor after the alleged act, there was nothing in the medical report as to the age of the girl. The defence counsel contended that the girl was 18 years when the offence was committed. He pointed out that the doctor who examined the girl did not indicate the age of the girl.
Held *inter alia*:

> I agree the doctor who examined should have indicated the age of the girl on the medical report but his omission to do so was in no way prejudicial to the prosecution since there is the evidence of the mother about the age of her daughter. Also by common sense the assessor and court were of the firm view that the victim was under 18 years. In the premises the prosecution has proved this ingredient.

Proof of age by observation by the court

In *Uganda v Onencan Willy Innocent* Criminal Session Case No. 0303/2000 the High Court held: A court can make a finding as to the age of the victim of defilement based on its observation of the victim in court.

In *Katima John v Uganda* Cr Appeal 23/1999. Court of Appeal for Uganda it was held that 'A trial judge is entitled to form her/his opinion about the age of a victim of defilement, through observation of the victim in court.'

Proof of age through court observation: common sense

CASE: *Uganda v Nsubuga Daniel* Criminal Session Case No. 338/97 High Court
The accused was convicted under Section 123 of the Uganda Penal Code. The issue was whether the victim was under 18 years.

The defence submitted that the prosecution failed to prove that the girl was under 18 years because there was no document to that effect. That, furthermore, although the mother and father of the victim came to court they never gave evidence. Instead, PW3 a sister to the victim testified in the case. According to the defence, the evidence of PW3 was hearsay.

The court **held** *inter alia* that it was enough for the court and the assessors to determine that the complainant before them was obviously under the age of 18 years and this was possible by common sense. It was not necessary for the prosecution to labour to prove that the complainant was below 18 years. Though the parents did not testify as to the age of the complainant, by common sense the court came to the conclusion that the complainant was far below the age of 18 years. There was evidence to prove age.

Note: the victim testified that she was about 8 years.

Unavailability for cross-examination of doctor who recorded age of victim not fatal to prosecution case

CASE: *Uganda v Twinomujuni Glazio* Criminal Session Case No. 57/98 High Court. The accused was prosecuted for defilement. In order to prove the age of the victim the prosecution relied on two witnesses. The first was the complainant herself who testified that she was 21 years old at the time of the trial. She had never gone to school. She did not know when she was born. Since the trial took place 6 years after the incident court concluded that if her testimony was correct she would have been 15 years at the time of the offence. The second piece of evidence relied upon by the prosecution in regard to proof of age was the report of the doctor who examined the victim after the sexual incident. The doctor recorded the age of the victim as about 15 years. Unfortunately by the time of the trial the doctor had died. Counsel for the defence argued that since the doctor was not available for cross-examination, his report could not be relied on.

The trial judge said *inter alia*:

- Cross examination of a doctor would not change a finding of fact recorded by the doctor through the application of medical science. I thus see no merit in the defence counsel's argument.
- Court had observed the witness in court and came to the conclusion that at the time of trial she was about 20 years.

Conclusion: Court can make a finding of age based on its observation of the witness. Even if the doctor who examined the victim and recorded her age was not available for cross-examination, that in itself was not fatal to the case.

Where defence concedes to girl being under 18 years there is no need for prosecution to prove fact of age

CASE: *Uganda v Rurahukayo John* Criminal Session Case No. 260/97 High Court
After the complainant gave her evidence in-chief, counsel for the accused suggested:

> I think the indictment should be amended to read defilement (and not rape) since the prosecutrix has said she was 16 years.

The trial judge allowed the indictment to be amended under Section.48 of the Trial on Indictment Decree.[8] The amended indictment was read to the accused. He pleaded not guilty.

The judge **held** *inter alia*:

> By suggesting and conceding that the indictment be amended to one of Defilement, counsel for the defence was conceding to the victim being 16 years and therefore below 18 years at the time the offence was committed. …the defence … made an express admission that Namanya (the victim) was 16 years. In the case of *Maama Agondoa v B.M. Kakiza* (1974) HCB 72 Justice Asthana made an observation.

> 'Having admitted in the written statement of defence that the accident did occur at the material time, date and place averred in the plaint, it did not lie in the mouth of the defendant or the driver to deny the occurrence of the accident.' That passage is relevant to the present case where the defence counsel made an admission, and later sought to challenge it by asking the prosecution to prove the age of the complainant. I … invoke the doctrine of Estoppel to hold that the defence cannot go back on their word and challenge the age of the complainant as not being 16 years at the time of the assault. Refer to section 113 of the Evidence Act and in the matter of M/S Kayondo & Co. Advocates High Court Civil Appeal No. 8/95.

Note however that the Judge further said that he had not decided on the age of the victim on the basis of the defence admission but that the admission, apart, he was persuaded by the evidence of the complainant, of the complainants mother as well as of the medical doctor who examined the complainant.[9]

Nevertheless, even where the defence concedes the age of the victim, the court must make a finding on it.

Factors which may guide court on the issue of age

In *Uganda v Baturine Richard* Criminal Session Case No. 589/96 the High Court held that where the defence does not contest the age of the complainant and the prosecution has presented evidence that the alleged victim was below 18 years at the time of the alleged sexual intercourse, the court is entitled to conclude that the ingredient of age has been proved beyond reasonable doubt.

In *Uganda v Rashid Busasi* Criminal Session Case No. 419/95 High Court, in determining the age of the victim the judge was guided by the following :

1. The parents' testimony
2. Medical reports
3. The judge's own observation of the victim in court.

Consent to sexual intercourse is no defence to a charge of defilement

The offence of defilement is based on the assumption that a person under a certain age is not capable of making rational, informed decisions about sex. The law steps in to make the decisions for the child.

CASES AND RULINGS

In *Nakholi v Republic* [1967] EA 337 Court of Appeal for East Africa it was held that consent to sexual intercourse affords no defence to a man on a charge of carnal knowledge of a girl under the age of consent.

In *Uganda v Rurahukayo John* Criminal Session Case 260/97 High Court cited with approval the case of *Uganda v Enoch Bampabura* Criminal Session Case No. 135/92 where it was held that 'it was no defence to a charge of defilement that the victim was of marriageable age or that she consented.'

Further cited with approval was *Uganda v Joseph Mulindwa* (1975) HCB 206 wherein it was *inter alia* held: 'consent is irrelevant in cases of defilement ... [an underage girl] is presumed to be incapable of consenting to sexual intercourse...' Consent of the victim is no defence to the offence of defilement.

See also *Uganda v Mugoya Wilson* Criminal Session Case No. 170/93 High Court[10] where it was held *inter alia* that the consent of the victim in this type of crime is not a defence.

In *Eria Ngobi v R* (1953) 20 EACA 154 Court of Appeal for Eastern Africa the appellant was charged with rape of a girl aged about 7 years. He was convicted of indecent assault under Section 122 of the Uganda Penal Code. The court held *inter alia*:

> Having regard to the age of the girl it was surprising that the indictment was laid under Section 117 and not under Section 123 of the Code, for in the latter case the element of consent is not open to the defence.

See also *Tumuhairwe Vincent v Ug* Criminal Appeal No. 29/97 where the Court of Appeal for Uganda held *inter alia* that in a defilement case, the consent of the child is no defence.

Evidence

Whereas normally in sexual offences the evidence of the victim is the best evidence on the issue of penetration and even identification, where this is not available, other cogent evidence can suffice to prove these facts.

Absence of medical evidence on penetration not necessarily fatal to prosecution case in defilement

CASE: *Bassita Hussein v Uganda* Criminal Appeal No. 35/1995 Supreme Court
The court **held** that:

- The act of sexual intercourse or penetration may be proved by direct or circumstantial evidence.
- Sexual intercourse is proved by the victims' own evidence and corroborated by medical or other evidence.
- Though desirable it is not a hard and fast rule that the victim's evidence and medical evidence must always be adduced in every case of defilement to prove sexual intercourse or penetration.
- Whatever evidence the prosecution may wish to adduce to prove its case; such evidence must be such that it is sufficient to prove the case beyond reasonable doubt.'

Absence of victim's evidence not necessarily fatal to prosecution case in sexual offences

In a defilement case, an accused can be convicted of the crime on the basis of testimony by witnesses other than the victim, e.g. medical evidence, eyewitnesses, etc. (*Rugarwana Fred v Uganda* Criminal Appeal No.39/95 Supreme Court)

Identification of accused proved without testimony of victim in defilement

CASE: *Uganda v Mugisha Afranco* Criminal Session Case No. 69/99 High Court
The accused was indicted for defiling a four-year-old girl. At the trial which took place almost two years later, the child victim was unable to testify. A *voire dire* had been conducted and the judge was of the view that she did not understand the duty of an oath and was not possessed of sufficient intelligence to understand the duty of telling the truth.

Issue: Whether or not, without the direct testimony of the victim as to the identity of her assailant, it can be proved beyond reasonable doubt that it was the accused who had sexual intercourse with her.

The judge cited with approval, *Badru Mwidu v Uganda* (Criminal Appeal No. 1/1997 where the victim of sexual assault was aged five years but at the time of the trial was out of the country undergoing treatment). The Uganda Court of Appeal **held**:

> ... where there is sufficient and cogent evidence to support a conviction, the trial court is entitled to act on such evidence notwithstanding the absence of the victim's evidence.
> ... whereas normally in sexual offences the evidence of the victim is the best evidence on issues of penetration and even identification, other cogent evidence can suffice to prove such facts in absence of that best evidence so identification of an accused is one of the facts that can be proved without testimony of a victim of defilement.

> Secondly the victim of this defilement reported to her mother the identity of her assailant and Uganda Court of Appeal in *Badru Mwidu* had this to say: 'Another point taken by Counsel for the appellant was that the evidence of PW4 to whom the victim in that case had first reported to, was hearsay. We do not agree. The evidence of a complainant by the victim of a sexual offence is admissible'. So, our starting point in determining the identity of the person who defiled the victim is her report to her mother that it was the accused who had defiled her. She mentioned his name ...

On the issue of sexual intercourse, the court relied on the following:
1. The mother of the victim who testified that she observed her daughter crying and walking with difficulty; she observed some semen on the victim's dress and some semen dripping from the victim's private parts.
2. Another woman (non-medical) who examined the victim immediately after the mother's complaint.
3. Medical examination at a hospital.

In the words of the judge: 'The victim's examination at the hospital confirmed what the two ladies had found, i.e. that the girl had had sexual intercourse with a man.'

Evidence of a child of tender age
Who is a child of tender years?
A discussion of defilement necessitates focus on evidential rules regarding the testimony of a child of tender years. In *Kibangeny Arap Kolil v R* [1959] EA 92 the Court of Appeal for East Africa defined a 'child of tender years' as follows:

In the absence of special circumstances, any child of any age, or apparent age, of under fourteen years, is a child of tender years.

CASE: *Patrick Akol v Uganda* Criminal Appeal No. 23/92 Supreme Court
The judge cited with approval *Kibangeny Arap Kolil v R* (1) [1959] EA 92 (Court of Appeal) and said that in the absence of special circumstances any child of an age or apparent age of under 14 years must be held to be a child of tender years, although essentially it remained a matter of the good sense of the court.

> Whether a child is of tender years is a matter for the good sense of the court and though it may be difficult to decide when a child understands the obligation of an oath, a court probably would have no difficulty in deciding whether he or she was of tender years. There can be no hard and fast line. There may be exceptional circumstances. But as a general rule, whenever a child appears to be around the age of 14 years or below, the Court should alert itself to the possibility that the child might not be of sufficient intelligence or be able to understand the nature of the oath, and should accordingly carry out a *voire dire* examination.

CASE: *Remigious Kiwanuka v Uganda* Criminal Appeal No. 41/95 Supreme Court
The complainant was 13 years at the time of the assault but was 15 years of age at the time of giving evidence. The Supreme Court held that consequently she was not a child of tender years and thus her evidence did not require corroboration on that score.

Note: It is worth noting that under the Children Act[11] the minimum age of criminal responsibility is 12 years. The question to be answered therefore is: since a person aged 12 years is considered old enough to understand the consequences of his/her conduct and can thus be held responsible for unlawful conduct, why should such a child be considered a child of tender years for purposes of giving evidence in a case where he/she is not the accused?

Victims of defilement are often children of tender years. And in many cases the only other witness (apart from the victim) to the act of defilement is another child of tender years. The rule on corroboration in sexual offences makes proof of cases in sexual offences difficult. In sexual offences where the victim is a child of tender years, evidential rules make the prosecution case doubly difficult – there is need to corroborate the testimony of the complainant in a sexual offence; there is need to corroborate the evidence of a child of tender years who gives evidence not on oath. The need to corroborate the evidence of a child of tender years is based upon the view that the evidence of a child is inherently less reliable than that of adults and that there is a grave danger of false accusations by children. It is assumed that children are highly imaginative and that their stories may be the product of suggestions by others.

It is perhaps not in doubt that the rules of evidence that undervalue and discredit the evidence of children exacerbate the difficulties of proof. It is also noted that the court atmosphere which is alien to the child may traumatise her/him further and inhibit the child from testifying. Coupled with the inequalities of power between the abusing adult and the abused child, it is likely that a great number of offenders escape conviction.

In *Uganda v Baturine Richard* Criminal Session Case No.589/96 the High Court stated:

> ... The evidence of a child of tender age ... requires corroboration. And where a child of tender age is the complainant in a sexual offence, her evidence doubly requires corroboration. Where the accused denies the charge, the prosecution must discharge its legal duty of proving each and every essential ingredient of defilement against the accused. ... an accused person does not bear the responsibility of proving his or her innocence. He or she cannot be convicted on account of the weakness of his or her defence or even absence of it. He or she can only be convicted upon the strength of the evidence adduced ...

In *Patrick Akol v Uganda* Criminal Appeal No. 23/92 the Supreme Court of Uganda adopted the definition of a 'child of tender years' given by the Court of Appeal for East Africa above. In the case of *Kibangeny Arap Kolil* above, the Supreme Court also laid out the procedure to be adopted in accepting the testimony of a child of tender years. The court cited Section 38 (3) of the Trial on Indictments Decree which provides as follows:

> Where, in any proceedings any child of tender years called as a witness does not, in the opinion of the court, understand the nature of an oath, his evidence may be received though not given on oath, if, in the opinion of the court, he is possessed of sufficient intelligence to justify the reception of the evidence, and understands the duty of speaking the truth.

> Provided that where evidence admitted by virtue of this subsection is given on behalf of the prosecution, the accused shall not be liable to be convicted unless such evidence is corroborated by some other material evidence in support thereof implicating him.

Conclusion: Where a child of tender years does not understand the nature of an oath, but is intelligent enough to understand the duty of speaking the truth, he/she nevertheless be allowed to testify in a court of law.

However the evidence of such a child must be corroborated by some other evidence before a conviction can be based on it.

What is a *voire dire*?

Courts around the world have historically employed special inquiries to assess whether or not children are competent to testify. The goal of the inquiry is to deterine if a child has the intellectual ability/competence to give evidene. The test of competency requires that the witness has sufficient intelligence, understanding and ability to observe in order to recall and communicate information, comprehend the seriousness of taking an oath, and appreciate the necessity of telling the truth. It is this inquiry in regard to a child witness that is called a *voire dire* process. The purpose of the process is to ascertain that the child:

1. knows the difference between truth and lies.
2. is prepared to testify truthfully; and
3. is capable of observing, remembering and verbally describing events.

Conducting a *voire dire*

The Court of Appeal for East Africa set out the procedure to be adopted where the court is confronted with a child of tender years called to give evidence. The procedure is that the judge should himself question the child to ascertain whether he or she understands the nature of an oath and if the judge does not allow the child to be sworn he should record whether or not in the opinion of the court, the child is possessed of sufficient intelligence to justify the reception of the evidence and if the child understands the duty of telling the truth.

Thus where a child's evidence is received without an oath, then the conviction cannot be sustained, unless there is corroboration by some other material evidence implicating the accused person.

CASE: *Kato Sula v Uganda* Criminal Appeal No. 25/2000 Supreme Court
The Supreme Court clearly set out the correct procedure in conducting a *voire dire*. The court said *inter alia*:

1. The inquiry, which is conducted before a child of tender years is questioned, is intended to test the child's capacity to understand the difference between truth and falsehood. A trial judge's note should reflect this …. There are two ways of recording proceedings in respect of voire dire. The first would be for the trial judge to write down a question put by the judge followed by the answer to each question. The answer must be written in the first person singular in the words spoken by the witness. Questions and answers are put in a dialogue form. The conclusions of the judge are made after that dialogue.

   The second practice is not to record the questions put by the judge but write down in a first person singular and in a narrative form the answers given by the young witness leaving the questions out unless a particular question must be recorded. Thereafter the trial judge records his conclusions. [see also *Gabriel s/o Maholi v R* [1960] EA 159]

   In the present case the trial court recorded the procedure as follows:
   Voire dire
   Court: Questions put to the young witness about whether or not she understands the nature of oath. She does not.
   Court: Questions put to test intelligence of young witness and capacity to tell the truth. She says that those who tell lies go to hell. She understands the duty of telling the truth. She will therefore give an unsworn testimony.
   The court pointed out that the procedure adopted was not quite correct.

2. The second issue was whether or not a child witness who gives evidence not on oath is liable to cross-examination. There appears to be a widespread misconception that a child witness who is allowed to give evidence without oath because of immature age should not or cannot be cross-examined after such child has testified. This is reflected in the judgment of the learned Justices of the Court of Appeal. (This) is erroneous … those children should be cross-examined to test the veracity of their evidence. … it would be unfair to any accused person to allow a child of tender years whose imagination can make that child to say whatever comes to its mind for the testimony of that child to go on court record and be acted upon without subjecting the evidence to cross examination. … even with the availability of whatever corroboration, evidence against any accused person which is allowed by court to go without cross-examination, is fraught with the danger of resulting in injustice.

CASE: *Fransisco Matovu v R* [1961] EA 260 Court of Appeal for East Africa.

In a case of murder, one of the witnesses was a boy of eight years old who was permitted to give unsworn evidence but there was no finding on the record as to the boy's intelligence or his understanding of the duty to tell the truth, nor was there anything indicating a direction to the assessors or to the judge himself that the boy's evidence required corroboration. The Court of Appeal commented about the issue and held *inter alia*:

1. A judge when confronted with a child of tender years called to give evidence, should himself question the child to ascertain whether he or she understands the nature of an oath and, if he does not allow the child to be sworn, he should record whether, in the opinion of the court, the child is possessed of sufficient intelligence to justify the reception of the evidence and understands the duty of telling the truth.

2. Where the child is a prosecution witness, the judge should also direct the assessors and himself that the child's evidence requires corroboration.

Failure/neglect to conduct a Voire Dire does not necessarily invalidate the testimony of a child of tender years

CASE: *Rugarwana Fred v Uganda* Criminal Appeal No. 39/95 Supreme Court

The appellant was convicted of defilement. It was alleged that he had sexual intercourse with a 5 year-old girl (PW1). PW2 found the appellant in the act of having sexual intercourse with PW1. PW2 reported the matter to PW3, a neighbour. On appeal it was contended that:

- The conviction was without sufficient corroboration.
- The judge did not conduct a *voire dire* before receiving the evidence of PW1 (the victim), a child of tender years.

Held *inter alia:*

1. Failure/neglect to conduct a *voire dire* does not necessarily invalidate the testimony of a child of tender years. If the child is possessed of sufficient intelligence to understand the duty of speaking the truth, her evidence can be relied upon.

On corroboration the supreme court said:

2. Corroboration of the child victim's testimony was found in the evidence of PW2 and PW3 with regard to the identity of the accused and the act of defilement. **Note:** The testimony of other witnesses can act as corroboration of the victim's story.

3. Medical evidence to the effect that the doctor found male sperms in the victim's vagina also offered corroboration of the fact of defilement.

4. In the view of the court, even if the evidence of PW1 (the victim) was to be ignored, the evidence of PW2 (the eyewitness) and PW3 (the neighbour to whom a report was made) together with the medical evidence would be sufficient to justify the conviction of the appellant.

CASE: *Sakila v Republic* [1967] EA 403 High Court of Tanzania

The complainant in a sexual assault case as well as two other witnesses were schoolgirls. When the complainant came to give her evidence the learned magistrate made the following comment: 'The witness is a girl of twelve years and the court explained to her the importance of evidence on oath.' She was then sworn in as a Christian.

In the case of the other witness the magistrate made the following comment: 'The witness is informed of the importance of giving evidence on oath.' She was found to be a young female person and sworn as a Christian.

In relation to the remaining witness the magistrate observed 'the witness was informed of the importance of giving evidence on oath and she knows to speak the truth'.

The appeal court **held** that the procedure adopted by the trial court in admitting evidence of witnesses of tender years was wrong. A trial court should examine a witness to satisfy itself that:

> The witness is possessed of sufficient intelligence and understands the duty of speaking the truth; (b) understands the nature of an oath. If satisfied as to (a) but not as to (b) the evidence may be received but not on oath; if satisfied as to (a) and (b) evidence should be taken on oath.

Justice Platt noted in his judgement that:

> The *voire dire* examination of the witnesses was almost, if not entirely, non-existent. The ages of two of the witnesses were not recorded. The witnesses were described as 'young persons'. It is difficult to say whether the witnesses were of tender years. On record the magistrate informed the witnesses of the importance of their giving evidence on oath. There is nothing to show that he satisfied himself that the witnesses themselves understood the nature of the oath.

Corroboration and children of tender years
When does evidence of a child of tender years require corroboration?

In *Uganda v Mukasa Everisto* Criminal Session Case No. 22/98 High Court it was **held** *inter alia:*

Corroboration

(a) In a sexual offence the evidence of the complainant must as a matter of practice be corroborated by some other independent testimony rendering it probable that the story of the complainant is true.

(b) The evidence of a child of tender years, if not on oath, requires corroboration. It can thus not afford corroboration on its own to the evidence of another child's evidence.

(c) Corroboration in sexual offences may be found in direct or circumstantial evidence accepted by the court and uncontradicted.

(d) The court having warned itself of the dangers pertaining to uncorroborated evidence may still convict if satisfied that the victim in a sexual offence is truthful.

The testimony of a child of tender years cannot corroborate the testimony of another child of tender years

CASE: *Uganda v Godfrey Agudi* Criminal Session Case No. 02/97 High Court

The accused was charged with defiling PW2. The prosecution's case was that PW2 (the victim) and PW3 were taken to the house of the accused, by the accused. The accused allowed PW3 (a 7 year-old boy) to leave but retained PW2. PW3 left but when he heard PW2 (his sister) scream he came back and found the accused on top of PW2.

On the act of sexual intercourse, both PW2 and PW3 testified. It was held by the judge that since PW2 and PW3 were children of tender years, who gave unsworn testimony, their testimony required corroboration. On top of all this, defilement being a sexual offence, the rule of practice is that it is unsafe to found a conviction based on the uncorroborated testimony of the complainant.

Corroboration of evidence of child

CASE: *Uganda v Swaibu Kyobe* Criminal Session Case No. 427/96 High Court

The accused was indicted for defilement. He denied the offence. The only eyewitness to the alleged act of sexual intercourse was the victim, aged 4 years on the relevant date.

In regard to the issue of corroboration the judge said that

1. Owing to the age (tender age) of the victim, her evidence must be corroborated as a matter of law (Section 38(3) of the T.I.D., *Kipageny Arap Kolil v R* [1959] EA 92 and *Patrick Akol Kolil vs Uganda* SCCA No. 23/94, reported in 1994 iv KALR 66)

2. Secondly, since the complainant is a complainant in a sexual offence, her evidence also requires corroboration, as a matter of practice.

The judge found corroboration in the evidence of the victim's mother who heard the victim cry, went to her and observed what she thought was a man's semen on the victim's knickers. She examined the victim's private parts and observed that they were swollen and torn at the lower end. She noted that the victim could not walk.

He also found corroboration in the medical report. All this led the judge to conclude that the prosecution had proved the ingredient of sexual intercourse beyond reasonable doubt:

- Conduct, in my view, was not the conduct of an innocent person. It amounts to circumstantial evidence, sufficient to corroborate the complainant's evidence that it was, the accused person who ravished her (*Uganda v Abel Ochan* [1972] Vol. 1 ULR 13).

- Besides, the accused lied to the court when he denied that he knew the home of the complainant's mother or the mother and the complainant themselves, when, indeed, those were his very neighbours.

Sworn evidence of a child of tender years is capable of corroborating the evidence of the complainant

CASE: *Mukasa Everisto v Uganda* Criminal Appeal No. 43/2000 Supreme Court:

Where a child of tender years gives evidence on oath, corroboration of her evidence as such witness is not necessary

CASE: *Bangirana v Uganda* [1975] HCB 361

The appellant was convicted of indecent assault on a female contrary to Section 122 (1) of the Uganda Penal Code. After conducting a *voire dire*, the sworn evidence of a girl aged 12 years was permitted by the trial magistrate.

It was held by the High Court that despite the fact that the girl was a child of tender years, her sworn evidence was capable of corroborating the evidence of the complainant.

Evidence: conclusion

From the various cases cited above one can conclude that:

1. According to statutory law a person accused of a crime cannot be convicted on the unsworn evidence of a child of tender years unless the testimony of such child is corroborated in some material particular by other evidence.

2. According to case law there is a rule of practice to the effect that the trial judge should warn the assessors and himself that although they may convict on the sworn evidence of a child witness, it would be dangerous to do so in the absence corroborative evidence.

Inconsistencies and contradictions in defilement

Unlike adult witnesses, children of tender years should not generally be expected to be completely consistent in their evidence. Allowances may be made for the state of their memory and for their possibly incomplete understanding of the situation.

In *Uganda v Twinomujuni Johnson* Criminal Case No. 191/98 High Court it was **held**:

> As it has been stated in several cases grave inconsistencies or contradictions in the witness's testimony, unless satisfactorily explained or reconciled will usually but not necessarily result in the evidence of a witness being rejected. Minor inconsistencies and contradictions will not normally have that effect unless they point to deliberate untruthfulness.

In the defilement case before court, Justice Kagaba attributed the inconsistencies to the age of the victim 'whose perception of events during the assault could not be mathematically accurate.

See also *Uganda v Ndosire* [1988-90] HCB 46; *Ssekitoleko v R* [1967] EA 532; *Uganda v Col Dusman Sabuni* [1981]HCB 13 and [1982] HCB1 and *Uganda v Abdalla Nassur* [1982] HCB1.

Conclusion

As already mentioned, the offence of defilement of under-age girls is based on an assumption that a person under a certain age (18 years) is not capable of making rational decisions about sex. Consequently, criminal law comes in to fix a minimum age of consent to sex. The law's role is, however, best understood if the offence of defilement is placed within the context of the human rights of children.

International human rights law recognises that childhood is 'entitled to special care and protection', and that a child, by reason of physical and mental immaturity, needs special protection, including legal protection. More specifically, both the African Charter on the Rights and Welfare of the Child as well as the United Nations Convention on the

Rights of the Child oblige states parties to protect children from sexual abuse and sexual exploitation. For example, Article 19 of the UN Child Convention provides that:

States Parties shall take all appropriate legislative...measures to protect the child from all forms of abuse...or exploitation, including sexual abuse.

In a similar vein, the African Child Charter provides under its Article 16 that:

States Parties to the Charter shall take specific legislative, administrative, social and educational measures to protect the child from all forms of abuse...including sexual abuse.

And under Article 34 of the UN Child Convention it is stated that:

States Parties undertake to protect the child from all forms of sexual exploitation and sexual abuse. For these purposes, States Parties shall in particular take all appropriate measures to prevent

(a) The inducement...of a child to engage in any unlawful sexual activity.

Similarly, Article 27 of the African Child Charter states that:

States Parties to the present charter shall undertake to protect the child from all forms of sexual exploitation and sexual abuse and shall in particular take measures to prevent the inducement, coercion or encouragement of a child to engage in any sexual activity.

Furthermore, under Article 21 (2) of the Charter it is provided that:

Child marriage...of girls and boys shall be prohibited and effective action, including legisation shall be taken to specify the minimum age of marriage to be 18 years.

As seen above, the provisions in the two child rights instruments call upon governments to *inter alia* use the law to protect children from sexual abuse and sexual exploitation. The Criminal Law of defilement is an example of such efforts. In Article 34 of the Convention and Article 27 of the Charter, it is implicit that consent by the child cannot be a defence. It is for this reason that both provisions oblige governments to protect the child, not only from coercion (force) but also from inducement (persuasion) and encouragement into sexual activity. The notion that governments protect children from non-coercive means of being lured into sexual activity is in line with the criminal law of defilement, which renders the child's consent to sexual intercourse a nullity.

---

1. Originally Section 123.
2. The death sentence is only the maximum possible sentence. It is not mandatory.
3. Before the 1990 amendment Section 123 (3) provided that: It shall be a sufficient defence to any charge under this section if it shall be made to appear to the court … that the person charged had reasonable cause to believe that the girl was of or above the age of 14 years.
4. Now Section 19.
5. Confirmed by the Court of Appeal. Although the case went to the Supreme Court on further appeal the holdings mentioned here were not over turned.
6. Chapter 248 Laws of Uganda (Revised) Edition.

7. Chapter 252 Laws of Uganda (Revised) Edition.
8. Now Trial on Indictments Act, Chapter 23 Laws of Uganda (Revised Edition) 2000.
9. Note: Although there was an appeal against both conviction and sentence (*John Rurahukayo v Uganda* Cr. Appeal No. 122 of 1999) the appeal against conviction was abandoned.
10. Confirmed by the Court of Appeal. Although the case went to the Supreme Court on further appeal the holdings mentioned here were not over turned.
11. Chapter 59 Laws of Uganda (Revised Edition) 2000.

7

Defilement of Persons with Mental Disabilities: Section 130 of the Uganda Penal Code Act[1]

Section 130 of the Uganda Penal Code states:

> Any person who, knowing a woman or girl to be an idiot or imbecile,[2] has or attempts to have unlawful carnal knowledge of her under circumstances not amounting to rape, but which prove that the offender knew at the time of the commission of the offence that the woman or girl was an idiot or imbecile, is guilty of a felony and is liable to imprisonment for fourteen years.[3]

It is noted that the substantive crime of defiling an idiot and the attempt to commit the crime are created by the same section and that the maximum sentence for either of the offences is the same.

Proofs

The prosecution has to prove the following ingredients:
1. Mental state of woman; imbecility or idiocy.
2. Carnal knowledge of the woman
3. Knowledge by the offender that woman is an imbecile/idiot

Defences

Just as in the case in defilement of girls under the age of 18 years, the law presumes that an imbecile or idiot is not capable of giving *meaningful* consent to sexual intercourse. It is for this reason that consent to sexual intercourse by a female of the relevant mental status affords no defence to the man. As noted by Card, Cross and Jones[4] the justification for the law is the need to protect women who, while they may understand the nature of the act, are easily open to persuasion and exploitation because of their mental defectiveness.

The two available defences are:
- Marriage
- Lack of knowledge of the woman's mental state.

CASE: *Ashabaruhanga Patrick v Uganda* Criminal Appeal No. 96/2000 Court of Appeal for Uganda

The appellant was indicted and convicted for defiling an idiot/imbecile.

The prosecution case was that the appellant had sexual intercourse with the complainant. The complainant immediately informed her cousin PW6. PW6 informed the parents of the complainant. The following day a group of people went to the home of the appellant but when the appellant saw the people he ran away. On medical examination, the doctor recorded the age of the complainant as 17 years. It was recorded that her hymen had been ruptured some time earlier. The doctor also indicated that the complainant was clearly mentally retarded.

The appellant denied the offence and set up an alibi. He appealed against conviction *inter alia* on the ground that the conviction was in the absence of evidence that the complainant was an idiot or imbecile.

Held:
- Section 124 of the Code is for protection of women who are mentally defective.
- Where a charge is drawn under Section 124 of the Penal Code Act, the prosecution must prove that the woman was either an imbecile or an idiot to such an extent as to be incapable of looking after herself and consequently incapable of giving valid consent.
- It would not matter whether the defect was from birth or early childhood or acquired during later life.
- The medical evidence adduced should specify the degree of retardation in terms of mental age.
- The trial court must make a finding as to whether the victim is an imbecile/idiot in law. This is because there is a difference between idiocy in law and the term idiot as used in common parlance.

The Appeal Court observed that it is obvious that the complainant knew the appellant and was able to give coherent evidence in court. In the court's view 'she was not severely subnormal so as to be unable to give consent. When the appellant testified that he had always known the complainant as an idiot, we are of the view that he was using the term in common parlance and not according to its legal meaning. The learned trial judge was, therefore, wrong in failing to make a legal finding on whether she was an idiot or an imbecile within the meaning of the law.'

Note: There seem to be few prosecutions under the section. But in interpreting the words 'idiot' or 'imbecile', we can also be guided by Section 7 of the Sexual Offences Act (1956) of England. According to Card, Cross and Jones[5] the said section is to the effect that a 'a defective is a person suffering from a state of arrested or incomplete development of mind which includes severe impairment of intelligence and social functioning'. Citing *Hall* (1987) 86 Crim App Rep 159, Card, Cross and Jones continue to state that whether or not there is such severe impairment is to be measured against the standard of normal persons, and not against those of other mentally handicapped persons.

Carnal knowledge under circumstances not amounting to rape

Section 130 of the Uganda Penal Code deals with instances in which the accused has 'enticed' the woman into having sexual intercourse with him. It does not deal with 'forced' sexual activity. Where the man forces the woman into sexual intercourse such act would still be rape and thus Section 123 would be applicable. Proof beyond reasonable doubt that the sexual intercourse was without a woman's consent is difficult to establish even where the woman is of normal mental faculty. This ingredient is likely to be even more difficult to prove where the victim is of less than normal mental status.

Our discussion of rape also indicates that belief by the man that a woman is consenting offers a defence to a man who has sexual intercourse with a non-consenting woman. See the discussion on the *mens rea* of rape (p.9). Faced with circumstances which indicate the possibility that an idiot has been raped, it would be wise for the prosecution to charge the suspect with two alternative counts; one under section 123 and the other under section 130. Under such circumstances if the prosecution fails to prove absence of consent but is able to prove knowledge by the accused that the woman is an imbecile, court will convict the accused under Section 130.

This is an offence which is rarely prosecuted. Perhaps the lack of cases arises out of the fact that the 'victims' are incapable of making reports and yet, unlike children, are often left on their own.

---

1. Originally Section 130.
2. The use of the phrases idiots and imbeciles is derogatory and has been dropped in several jurisdictions. For example, under the Sexual Offences Act of 1956, England the equivalent section uses the phrases "a woman who is defective".
3. The law relating to defilement of idiots was left untouched by the 1990 Statute.
4. Criminal Law, 12th Edition. Butterworths. 1992.
5. Criminal Law, 12th Edition. Butterworths. 1992.

Introduction

Morality refers to principles of right and wrong, or good and bad behaviour in a given society. It is a code of conduct put forward by *a* society and it is expected that the behaviour of individuals is guided by the code. Consequently, conduct, which is condoned by society is considered moral whereas conduct which is abhorred or disapproved of is considered immoral. Card, Cross, and Jones (1992:18) state that 'a rule may be said to be one of social morality, when it is accepted by the bulk of a given society as laying down as standard behaviour to which its members ought to conform and as justifying severe censure for those who break it.'

A look at the Uganda Penal Code reveals that the phrase 'offences against morality' is used in reference to offences of a sexual nature. This is inspite of the fact that other forms of behaviour that, for example, violate other people's property (e.g theft) or that cause bodily injury to other persons (e.g assaults, homicide) are also contrary to accepted standards of behaviour and can thus be referred to as immoral. One can safely contend that in the context of the Uganda Penal Code, immorality is synonymous with sexual misconduct.

As indicated in the introduction to this book, some of the offences of a sexual nature violate 'accepted' norms of sexual behavior but do not infringe the rights of any particular individual. It is only such 'victimless crimes' that I have referred to as offences against morality and this chapter is focused on this category of offences.[1] I however find it necessary to note that the question whether criminal law should enforce morality is often the subject of intense debate. The criminalisation of conduct which is 'victimless' is sometimes challenged on the ground that morality as such is a private matter and that it is not the object of the criminal law to police private morality. For example, John Stuart Mill in his essay *On Liberty* stated that:

> The object of this Essay is to assert one very simple principle, as entitled to govern absolutely the dealings of society with the individual in the way of compulsion and control, whether the means used be physical force in the form of legal penalties, or the moral coercion of public opinion. That principle is, that the sole end for which mankind are warranted, individually or collectively in interfering with the liberty of action of any of their number, is self-protection. That the only purpose for which power can be rightfully exercised over any member of a civilized community, against his will, is to prevent harm to others. His own good, either physical or moral, is not a sufficient warrant. He cannot rightfully be compelled to do or forbear because it will be better for him to do so, because it will make him happier, because, in the opinions of others, to do so would be wise, or even right. These are good reasons for remonstrating with him, or reasoning with him, or persuading him, or entreating him, but not for compelling him, or visiting him with any evil, in case he do otherwise. To justify that, the conduct from which it is desired to deter him must be calculated to produce evil to someone else. The only part of the conduct of any one, for which he is amenable to society, is that which concerns others. In the part, which

merely concerns himself, his independence is, of right, absolute. Over himself, over his own body and mind, the individual is sovereign. (Library of Liberal Arts edition, p.13)[2]

And the Wolfenden Committee on Homosexual Offences and Prostitution also stated that the function of criminal law was 'To preserve public order and decency, to protect the citizen from what is offensive or injurious, and to provide sufficient safeguards against exploitation and corruption of others, particularly those who are specially vulnerable.' The report further emphasised that ' it is not ..... the function of the law to intervene in the private lives of citizens, or to seek to enforce any particular pattern of behavior, further than is necessary to carry out the purposes we have outlined.'[3]

According to the Committee, 'there must remain a realm of private morality which is not the law's business.'

However, contrary to the above opinions, some scholars opine that conduct, which is contrary to social morality, can be prohibited and punished by criminal law even though it does no harm to others. In the nineteenth century, Stephen in his book *Liberty, Equality, Fraternity*[4] stated that:

> there are acts of wickedness so gross and outrageous that, self-protection apart, they must be prevented as far as possible at any cost to the offenders, and punished, if they occur, with exemplary severity.

In line with Stephen's view Lord Devlin challenged the views of the Wolfenden Committee in his *The Enforcement of Morals,* London 1965.

According to Lord Devlin there are certain important social structures and institutions which a society is justified in protecting even at the cost of coercing individuals whose conduct threatens to undermine the said structures and institutions. Lord Devlin thus contends that consequently, a vital function of the criminal law is to enforce the generally shared moral values of a society that are associated with its important institutions. Devlin argues that a society's existence depends on the maintenance of shared political and moral values. He argues that violation of the shared morality loosens one of the bonds which hold a society together, and thereby threatens it with disintegration. Devlin further argues that the state has a claim to legislate on matters of morals when it has a need to preserve itself.   He contends that:

> A recognized morality is as necessary to society's existence as a recognized government ... and although a particular act of immorality may not harm or endanger or corrupt others, for we must not view conduct in isolation from its effect on the moral code .... It might threaten one of the great moral principles on which society is based.... In this sense the breach is an offence against society; as a whole ... this is why the suppression of vice is as much the law's business as the suppression of subversive activities.

The criminal law should thus, according to Devlin, be invoked to protect shared morality in the same way as it is used against other offensive behaviour.

Lord Devlin's view is also in line with what Lord Simonds asserted in the case of *Shaw v Director of Public Prosecutions* ([1962] AC 220, [1961] 2 All ER 446).

Shaw was charged with, inter alia, a conspiracy to corrupt public morals by publishing a booklet, *The Ladies' Directory,* which listed names, addresses and other information concerning prostitutes such as the sexual services they were willing to offer. The information was capable of helping an interested person to get in touch with a prostitute.

The Court of Criminal Appeal as well as the House of Lords upheld Shaw's conviction by the trial court. Lord Simonds of the House of Lords said:

> In the sphere of criminal law I entertain no doubt that there remains in the courts of law a residual power to enforce the supreme and fundamental purpose of the law, to conserve not only the safety and order but also the normal welfare of the state, and that it is their duty to guard it against attacks which may be the more insidious because they are novel and unprepared for.

Contrary to Devlin's and Simond's views, Professor HLA Hart (1907-92) supported the Wolfenden report thus:

> No doubt we would all agree that a consensus of moral opinion on certain matters is essential if society is to be worth living in. Laws against murder, theft and much else would be of little use if they were not supported by a widely diffused conviction that what these laws forbid is also immoral. So much is obvious. But it does not follow that everything to which the moral vetoes of accepted morality attach is of equal importance to society nor is there the slightest reason for thinking of morality as a seamless web; one which will fall to pieces carrying society with it, unless all its emphatic vetoes are enforced by law.

In reference to the arguments of Devlin and of Hart, the American jurist, Dwarkin has proposed that the attempt to differentiate acts that cause harm and those that do not ought to come to an end. Dwarkin argued that it is more important that attention be devoted to a consideration of a distinction between 'basic liberties' which ought *never* to be curtailed, save in the event of possible direct harm, and 'liberty in general', which *might* be curtailed, perhaps, if the effect would be to secure a gain in communal welfare as a whole.

Whatever the arguments from the various sides, Uganda's criminal law continues to penalise conduct which runs against social norms and values, even where no individual is injured by the prohibited conduct. As recently as 1990, prostitution, which had hitherto not been a crime, was criminalised. The 1990 amendment also raised the sentences for several offences of a sexual nature, which can be described as victimless crimes, for example incest between consenting adults and homosexual acts. It can thus be said that for now it is the views of scholars and jurists like Devlin which seem to prevail in Uganda's penal legislation.

1. Sexual offences which involve violence against and abuse of others have been referred to as sexual assaults and are the subject of an earlier discussion.
2. http://www.serendipity.li/jsmill/jsmill.htm Accessed on 3/29/2005
3. Report of Committee on Homosexual offences and Prostitution, British Government study, 1957
4. Cited in Card, Cross and Jones (1992:20)

9
Adultery: Section 154 Penal Code Act.[1]

Section 154 of the Uganda Penal Code creates the offence adultery.

1. Any man who has sexual intercourse with any married woman not being his wife commits adultery and is liable to imprisonment for a term not exceeding twelve months or to a fine not exceeding two hundred shillings; and, in addition, the court shall order any such man on first conviction to pay the aggrieved party compensation of six hundred shillings, and on a subsequent conviction compensation not exceeding twelve hundred shillings as may be so ordered.

2. Any married woman who has sexual intercourse with any man not being her husband commits adultery and is liable on first conviction to a caution by the court and on a subsequent conviction to imprisonment for a term not exceeding six months.

The law on adultery punishes a man who has sexual intercourse with a *married woman* who is not his wife; as well as a married woman who has sexual intercourse with a man who is not her husband.

It is imperative to note that the marital status of the man engaged in the sexual act is irrelevant. What is of relevance is the fact that the woman is married to a man other than the person with whom she has had sexual intercourse. Consequently:

1. Where a married man has sexual intercourse with an unmarried female, such conduct does not constitute criminal adultery.
2. Where a married woman has sexual intercourse with a married man, both are guilty of adultery.
3. Where a married woman has sexual intercourse with an unmarried man, both are guilty of adultery.

What has to be proved
Apart from some of the ingredients of any sexual offence – that penetration took place; that the accused was the actual perpetrator – the prosecution must also prove that the accused knew the woman was married to someone else. Consent by the woman is not a defence.

Lack of knowledge of woman's marital status is a defence on a charge of adultery
CASE: *Uganda v Nikolla and Another* [1966] EA 345 High Court
N and M were jointly charged with 'wilfully and unlawfully' committing adultery under Section 150, although the words 'wilfully' and 'unl;awfully' do not appear in the section. At the trial evidence was led that M was married to T according to native law and custom but that some years later she deserted her husband and rejoined her brother and that at the time of the alleged offence she lived with her brother. M testified that she had deserted T and had lived with her brother for 3 years before her marriage to N.

N's defence was that he came to know M for the first time when her brother offered her to him in marriage as an unmarried woman and that he married her with her consent according to native law and custom. The trial magistrate held that although N did not know that M was married, since M had not been legally divorced, N and M had committed adultery. The case came before the Chief Justice for revision and one issue was: whether Section 150 A created any absolute liability.

Held:
1. If a man and a woman are both charged with adultery, there should be separate counts because the *mens rea* in each case is different.
2. The absence of the word 'knowingly' or 'wilfully' from the section merely relieved the prosecution from proving knowledge or wilfulness on the part of the person charged with the offence and it was plain that the section did not contain an absolute prohibition of the offence of adultery; it was open to an accused person to show that in fact he did not know that the woman was married to any other person.

Judgement: An allegation that a man and woman committed adultery must carry the implication that the man having known that the woman was married to another man unlawfully had sexual intercourse with her. Similarly that the woman with the full knowledge that she was married to someone unlawfully had sexual intercourse with another man not her husband.

Conclusion: The prosecution does not need to prove knowledge by the accused but it is a defence for an accused to plead that he did not know that the woman was married.

CASE: *Alai v Uganda* [1967] EA 596

The adulterer and adulteress and her husband were all Moslems and the marriage between the adulteress and her husband was by Muslim rites.

Issue: Whether the offence of adultery applies to all types of marriage or whether it is restricted to monogamous marriages only and does not apply to potentially polygamous marriages (including Muslim marriages) because of the definition of 'husband' and 'wife' in Section 4 of the Penal Code Act.

Note: Under Section 4, 'husband' is defined as husband of a monogamous marriage. 'Wife' means wife of a monogamous marriage.

Held:
1. 'any married woman' in Section 150A means any woman who is married to any man irrespective of the form of marriage; provided that such marriage has been conducted in one of the forms recognised by the people of Uganda, including marriages according to the custom of the people.
2. Section 150A uses the words 'any married woman' so that the definition of 'wife' in S4 is not relevant.

In its judgement, the court also observed that the charge against the appellant as framed was bad in law. It did not disclose any offence. There was no allegation in the count that the woman named therein was a married woman, and that she was married to any particular person and in particular to the complainant.

The essence of the offence created by S 150 A(1) is that the man charged must have had sexual intercourse with a married woman not being his wife, that is to say, a woman married to another man. Merely having sexual intercourse with a woman not married to any one is not an offence within section 150A (1).

CASE: *Uganda v Andrew Keneth Otema-Opok* Criminal Revision 433 of 1970
The accused, a man and a woman were charged in 2 counts with adultery under Section 150A(1) and (2) of the Penal Code. The particulars in count 2 were that:'Janet ... had sexual intercourse with Andrew not being her husband.'
   The magistrate ordered the sale of accused 1's property in default of payment of the compensation of Shs 600 to the complainant.
Held:
   1. The particulars were defective because they did not allege that the woman was a married woman. No offence was committed by a woman under section 150A(2) unless she was married and had sexual intercourse with a man other than her husband. The accused said in answer to the charge 'Accused 1 had sexual intercourse with me.' She did not thereby admit that she was a married woman. The plea was equivocal and consequently her conviction based on it was bad in law.
   2. There was no provision in S.150 A (1) for ordering accused's property to be sold in default of payment of compensation. In the event of failure to pay the remedy appeared to be resort to the provisions of section 305 of the Criminal Procedure Code where the court might issue a warrant for levy. The order for sale was illegal and is set aside.

CASE: *Ayor and Another v Uganda* [1968] EA 303 High Court
The two accused, a man and a woman, were charged jointly with adultery. The woman pleaded 'guilty' and subsequently gave evidence against the man. Her evidence was uncorroborated and was the only evidence implicating the man. He was convicted. On revision:
Held:
   1. It is undesirable in adultery cases that both the man and the woman should be charged; but if they are both charged there should be separate counts. (*Uganda v Nikola* followed)
   2. The woman being an accomplice, her evidence being uncorroborated and it being the only evidence implicating the man, and the trial magistrate having failed to warn himself about this, his conviction could not stand.
In the judgement the High Court said *inter alia*:

> The kind of corroboration required is not confirmation of independent evidence of everything the accomplice relates, as his evidence would be unnecessary if that were so. What is required is some independent testimony which implicates the accused in some material particular ...

Punishments for adultery
A man who is convicted of adultery is dealt with differently from a woman who is convicted of adultery. The differences in treatment are I believe, based on gender stereotypes.

1. Women are not expected to have property whereas men are expected to be propertied. Thus, when dealing with a male offender, court has the discretion to choose between imprisonment on the one hand and a fine (monetary consequences) on the other. In dealing with a female offender, payment of money (a fine) is not an available option. It is perhaps because of this assumption that a female offender is either cautioned or imprisoned.

2. Women are more leniently handled as offenders and perhaps this is based on the assumption (stereotype) that women as the 'weaker sex' are enticed by men into sexual activity. Consequently, where a woman is a first offender the court will caution (warn) her. On the other hand, a male first offender can even end up in detention - this can be for as long as twelve months.

3. Compensation: A man who is convicted of adultery will be required to pay compensation to the aggrieved party – the husband of the woman with whom the offender has had sexual intercourse.[2] This requirement of the law is most probably based on the 'need' to protect male property in the female body. My argument is based on the fact that compensation in law is normally linked to the need to offset a loss/damage caused to one person's property by another. Compensation is usually awarded to restore the loss arising out of the wrongful act of another and thus as far as possible, put the victim in the position he would have been in, had the wrong doer not committed the wrongful act. Perusal of the Penal Code reveals that criminal law rarely calls for compensation. In the few cases where compensation is used in the Penal Code, the offences are offences against property (see Embezzlement Section 268; causing financial loss by person employed by Government, a bank, a credit institution, etc 269 and Robbery 268). Thus when the law requires an adulterer to pay money to the woman's husband, the question is: Is the husband being paid (compensated) for either loss of value or for trespass to his property? It appears that compensation is linked to a husband's proprietary rights in his wife's body. Within Uganda Society, this notion may be based on the practice of bride price – exchange of property from the man's family into the wife's family on marriage.

As already discussed a married woman will be convicted of adultery if she has sexual intercourse with a man other than her husband. The man in question may either be married or unmarried. It is noted that even when that man is married, the female offender will not be required to pay compensation to her lover's wife. It is thus assumed that a wife (a woman) has no proprietary interest in her husband's (a man's) body.

Sexual intercourse between a married man and an unmarried female

As already mentioned, a man is only guilty of adultery if he has sexual intercourse with another man's wife. A married man is not guilty of any offence if he has sexual intercourse with an unmarried woman. In light of the fact that Ugandan marriage law recognises polygamy[3] as a valid union and that most societies in Uganda are potentially polygamous, the law on criminal adultery is not surprising. The process of 'acquiring' a second and indeed any other subsequent wife involves courting and courting may translate into sexual intercourse before marriage. It is perhaps for this reason that in a society where men are given sexual freedom, a married man's extra-marital sexual intercourse with a woman who is not a wife to anybody is not frowned upon by the criminal law.

But it must be noted that the practice and law of polygamy is unconstitutional. It violates Article 31 of Uganda's Constitution, which provides that men and women are entitled to equal rights in marriage, during marriage and at its dissolution.

Uganda's Article 31 is in line with the Convention on the Elimination of all Forms of Discrimination against Women (CEDAW which also affirms the equality of human rights for women and men in society and in the family. Other earlier human rights conventions also confer equal rights on men and women in marriage.[4]

As I said elsewhere, perhaps there is no clearer way of emphasizing the law of male sex-rights than through the practice of polygamy. For as it has been argued by Mayambala (1996), polygamy is against the spirit of equality between men and women because it allows one spouse (the husband) unilaterally to fundamentally change the quality of the couple's family life. Further still, polygamy makes the husband and wife unequal partners in marriage by subjecting the wife to unconditional fidelity in the same way as her counterpart in a monogamous marriage, when the husband is under no reciprocal duty – the husband has an exclusive right to sex with each of his wives and yet the wives are prohibited from having sex with any other man.[5]

It is therefore no surprise that in the Protocol to the African Charter on Human and People's Rights on the Rights of Women in Africa, Article 6 enjoins States Parties to inter alia enact appropriate national legislative measures to guarantee that polygamy shall be prohibited.[6]

In its General Recommendation No. 21, the Committee on the Elimination of all forms of Discrimination against Women analysed Article 16 of the convention which accords women and men equality in all matters relating to marriage and the family. The committee's comments acknowledge that the form and concept of the family can vary from state to state, and even between regions within a state. It nevertheless stated that:

> Whatever form it takes and whatever the legal system, religion, custom or tradition within the country, the treatment of women in the family both at law and in practice must accord with the principles of equality and justice for all people, as Article 2 of the Convention requires.

Making specific mention of polygamy, the committee, under its comment 14(d) stated:

> States Parties' reports also disclose that polygamy is practiced in a number of countries. Polygamous marriages contravene a woman's right to equality with men, and can have such serious emotional and financial consequences for her and her dependants that such marriages ought to be discouraged and prohibited.

The Committee also noted with concern that some States Parties, whose constitutions guarantee equal rights, permit polygamous marriages in accordance with personal or customary law. According to the committee, this trend violates the concept of equality between the sexes and also breaches the provisions of Article 5 (a) of CEDAW, which enjoins States Parties to take all appropriate measures:

To modify the social and cultural patterns of conduct of men and women, with a view to achieving the elimination of prejudices and customary and all other practices which are based on the idea of the inferiority or the superiority of either of the sexes or on stereotyped roles for men and women.

And while discussing a report submitted to it by the Government of Gabon, the UN Human Rights Committee has deplored the practice of polygamy as incompatible with the principle of equality between men and women.

And more recently the UN Human Rights Committee while considering Uganda's initial report (CCPR/C/UGA/2003/1) at its meeting held on 31st March 2004 noted with concern the continued existence of customs and traditions in Uganda that affect the principle of equality of men and women that may impede the full implementation of many provisions of the covenant. According to the Committee it

deplores the fact that polygamy is still recognised by law in Uganda;... Polygamy is incompatible with equality of treatment with regard to the right to marry. The provisions in the proposed Domestic Relations Bill which would discourage the practice of polygamy are not sufficient.

The Committee called upon Uganda to take legislative measures to outlaw polygamy in addition to strengthening its ongoing awareness-raising campaigns.[7]

General Recommendations and concluding observations of the UN Committee mentioned above should be a guide to states like Uganda, which legally condone polygamy. Although as a formal matter of international law, general recommendations are not binding on States Parties, they are considered as particularly persuasive interpretations of it. Such interpretations can be invoked before courts and tribunals. By giving validity to a practice that has been declared contrary to the spirit of the International Covenant on Civil and Political Rights (CCPR) and of the Covenant on the Elimination of all forms of Discrimination Against Women (CEDAW) Uganda is acting contrary to its international obligations.

Constitutional issues on adultery: Hypothetical cases
CASE 1: *Uganda v Mukasa*
On the 1st October, 2004 Mukasa, a male aged 20 years is brought before a Grade 1 Magistrate. He is charged with having committed Criminal Adultery under section 154 of the Penal Code Act. According to the facts, Mukasa is married. On September 20th 2004 he was caught having sexual intercourse with an unmarried woman aged 20 years. The police arrested Mukasa at a hotel where he had spent a night with the young woman. The two were caught red-handed having sexual intercourse.
Issues:
The issues which the prosecution would have to prove would be
1. That Mukasa had sexual intercourse with a woman.
2. The woman in question must have been married to another man at the time of sexual intercourse with Mukasa
Holding
Since the woman with whom Mukasa had sexual intercourse was unmarried at the time, Mukasa cannot be convicted under Section 154.

Convicting Mukasa would violate Article 28(7) of the Constitution which provides that no person shall be charged with or convicted of a criminal offence which is founded on an act or omission that did not at the time it took place constitute a criminal offence.

CASE 2: *Uganda v Babirye*
On 1st October 2004, Babirye, a female aged 20 years is brought before a Grade 1 Magistrate. Babirye is charged under Section 154 of the Penal Code Act.

According to the facts, Babirye is married to one Opio. For months, Opio suspected that his wife was having a love affair with a young man Pinto. Pinto is unmarried. On 20th September 2004, Babirye was seen entering a hotel with Pinto. An hour later, the Police 'raided' the hotel and Babirye and Pinto were caught red-handed, having sexual intercourse.

Issues:
The issues which the prosecution had to prove were:
1. That Babirye had sexual intercourse with a man other than Opio.
2. That Babirye was at the time of the sexual intercourse, married to Opio.

Held:
Babirye is guilty of adultery.

It is clear that the ingredients constituting criminal adultery are different depending on whether the accused is male or female.

Observations
From the hypothetical cases above, it is clear that Section 154 treats women and men differently and that the different treatment is attributable to sex. The section is thus contrary to several articles of the Constitution – Articles 21, 31 and 33. The said constitutional articles provide for equality between men and women.
Article 21(1) provides:

> All persons are equal before and under the law in all spheres of political, economic, social and cultural life and in every other respect and shall enjoy equal protection of the law.

> 21(2) Without prejudices to clause (1) of this article, a person shall not be discriminated against on the ground of sex.

> (3) For purposes of this article, 'discriminate' means to give different treatment to different persons attributable only or mainly to their respective descriptions by *sex*, race, colour, ethnic origin, tribe, birth, creed or religion, or social or economic standing, political opinion or disability. (my emphasis)

Article 31 provides:

> 31(1) Men and Women of the age of eighteen years and above, have the right to marry and to found a family and are entitled to equal rights in marriage, during marriage and at its dissolution.

Article 33(1) provides:

> Women shall be accorded full and equal dignity of the person with men.

The criminal law of adultery gives more sexual freedom to men than it does to women.

Although the criminal law of adultery has not been challenged in a court of law for being unconstitutional, I am convinced that if a petition were to be brought before the Constitutional Court, the Court would declare section 154 unconstitutional. An analogy can be drawn from the declarations of the Constitutional Court in Constitutional Petition No. 2 of 2003[8] wherein several provisions of the Divorce Act were successfully challenged for perpetuating inequality between men and women. For purposes of the present discussion I will limit focus on Section 4 of the Divorce Act. Section 4(1) provides that:

> A husband may apply by petition to the court for the dissolution of his marriage on the ground that since the solemnization of the marriage his wife has been guilty of adultery.

> 4 (2): A wife may apply by petition to the court for the dissolution of her marriage on the ground that since the solemnisation of the marriage,

> (a) Her husband has changed his profession of Christianity for the profession of some other religion, and gone through a form of marriage with another women; or
> (b) has been guilty of -
>   (i)   incestuous adultery;
>   (ii) bigamy with adultery;
>   (iii) marriage with another women with adultery;
>   (iv) rape, sodomy or bestiality;
>   (v)   adultery coupled with cruelty; or
>   (vi) adultery coupled with desertion without reasonable excuse, for two years or upwards.

The petitioners submitted that Section 4 of the Divorce Act violated Articles 21, 31 and 33 because it made prescriptions for divorce on the basis of sex. The petitioners based their argument on the fact that the section allows a man to divorce only on proof of one ground whereas women are allowed to prove many grounds.It was argued that this causes hardship to a man who may have other grounds, other than adultery. It was also argued that on the other hand, the section compels the women to have to prove many grounds whereas the man is not required to do the same. For a man proof of adultery by his wife is in itself adequate ground for a divorce. For a woman whose husband has committed adultery, court will not grant divorce unless the adultery is accompanied by some other wrong such as cruelty.

Held *inter alia:*

The constitutional court unanimously declared:

> That Section 4 is derogation to articles 21, 31 and 33.

In the lead judgement of Twinomujuni J.A. Court declared that:

> (a) Section 4(1) of the Divorce Act contravenes and is inconsistent with Articles 21(1) & (2), Article 31(1) and Article 33(1) and (6) of the Constitution.
> (b) Section 4(2) of the Divorce Act contravenes and is inconsistent with Articles 21(1) & (2), Article 31(1) and Article 33(1) and (6) of the Constitution.

Twinomujuni J.A said:

> I have no doubt in my mind that the impugned provisions of our Divorce Act are a result of the Englishman's pre-20th century perceptions that a man was a superior being to a woman and they could not be treated as equals in marriage. It is, in my view, glaringly

impossible to reconcile the impugned provisions of the Divorce Act with our modern concepts of equality and non-discrimination between the sexes enshrined in our 1995 Constitution.

The similarity between the law on divorce dealt with by the Constitutional Court discussed above and the criminal law of adultery lies in the observation that the law's treatment of a person is solely dependent on whether the person is a man or a woman.

In the criminal law of adultery (Section 154) a married man who engages in sexual intercourse with an unmarried woman will be free of criminal sanctions. On the other hand his female counterpart (a married woman) will be a criminal if she has sexual intercourse with an unmarried man. The woman's behaviour is perceived differently from the man's behaviour, in a way which discriminates against the women.

It also follows that men have more rights than women during marriage, one such right being that a man has the freedom to engage in sex outside marriage without sanctions from the criminal law whereas the woman does not have such freedom. Such a law is thus null and void for being unconstitutional.

Note is made of the fact that the proposed Domestic Relations Bill (2003) has created a gender neutral offence of adultery. Under Section 62 it is provided that:

1. Where a party to a marriage has sex with a person other than his or her spouse, both parties to that sexual act commit the offence of adultery and each is, on conviction, liable to a fine not exceeding forty-eight currency points or imprisonment not exceeding two years or both.

2. A party convicted under subsection (1) is liable in addition to any criminal penalty, to pay compensation of an amount determined by the court -
    a) to his or her own spouse, if any;
    b) to the spouse, if any, of the other party to the offence.

---

1. Originally section 150 A.
2. Court cases which define aggrieved party will be discussed under the offence of elopement.
3. I use the term polygamy to refer to a situation where a man has more than one wife at the same time. Technically, polygamy refers to having a plurality of wives or husbands at the same time. It thus covers polygyny (the practice of a man having several wives at the same time) as well as polyandry (the practice of a woman having more than one husband at the same time.) My use of the term polygamy, instead of polygyny, is based on the fact that in Uganda, polygamy is popularly used in reference to polygyny. The popular usage has in fact been adopted by statute and thus, the Uganda Registration of Customary Marriages Decree, refers to the practice of a man having more than one wife, as polygamy. See also the Protocol to the African Charter on Human and People's Rights, and General Recommendation 14 of the Convention on the Elimination of All Forms of Discrimination Against Women (CEDAW). Both human rights instruments use the term polygamy to mean polygyny.
4. Article 2 of the Universal Declaratioin of Human Rights provides that everyone is entitled to all rights and freedoms set forth in this Declaration, without distinction of any kind such as sex and under Article 16 (1): Men and women are entitled to equal rights at marriage, during marriage and at its dissolution. According to the International convention on Civil and Political Rights, the States Parties undertake to ensure the equal rights of en and women to

the enjoyment of all civil and political rights (Article 3), while under Article 23 (4), States Parties are enjoined to take appropriate steps to ensure equality of rights of spouses during marriage. The Covenant on Economi, Social and Cultural Rights also undertakes to ensure the equal rights of me and women in the enjoyment of rights set forth in the Covenant. According to the African Charter on Human and People's Rights, discrimination on the ground of sex is prohibited and under Article 18 thereof, member states are called upon to eliminate every discrimination against women.

5. See Lillian Tibatemwa-Ekirikubinza: Gender and Human Rights: A Case Study of Polygamy among the Basoga of Uganda. Centre for Basic Research, Kampala. Working Paper No. 81/ 2003 ISBN 9970-516-80-9.

6. As adopted by the meeting of Government Experts in Addis Ababa on 16 November 2001. CAB/KEG/66.6/Rev.1)

7. See concluding observations of the Human Rights Committee, Uganda, UN Doc. CCPR/Co/ UGA (2004) at http://wwwl.umn.edu/humanits/hrcommittee/uganda 2004.htm/ Accessed on 23/2/2005.

7. Uganda Association of Women Lawyers, Dora Byamukama, Jacqueline Asiimwe Mwesige, Peter Ddungu Matovu, Joe Oloka-Onyango, Phillip Karugaba v The Attorney General.

10

Elopement:
Section 127 of the Uganda Penal Code Act[1]

In a prosecution for adultery, one of the ingredients that must be proved is sexual intercourse. Just as it is in any criminal trial the ingredient must be proved beyond reasonable doubt. In most cases of adultery, the man and woman involved in the sexual act are willing partners. This makes the work of the prosecution even harder. It is because of these practical difficulties that parliament created the offence of elopement.

Simply put, the offence of elopement occurs when a married person runs away with a lover.

Section 127

1. Any person who elopes with a married woman or entices or causes a married woman to elope with him commits an offence and is liable on conviction to imprisonment for a term not exceeding twelve months or to a fine not exceeding two hundred shillings; and, in addition, the court shall order any such person on first conviction to pay the aggrieved party compensation of six hundred shillings, and on a subsequent conviction compensation not exceeding twelve hundred shillings.

2. Any female who elopes with a married man or entices or causes a married man to elope commits an offence and is liable on first conviction to imprisonment for a term not exceeding twelve months or to a fine not exceeding two hundred shillings; and, in addition, the court shall order any such person on first conviction to pay the aggrieved party compensation of six hundred shillings, and on a subsequent conviction compensation not exceeding twelve hundred shillings.

3. Any person who agrees to elope with another person commits an offence and is liable on first conviction to a caution by the court and on a subsequent conviction to imprisonment for a term not exceeding six months or to a fine not exceeding six hundred shillings.

Under Section 127(1), the offender is a man and the offence committed is eloping with a married woman.

Under Section 127 (2), the offender is a female. The party she elopes with must be a married man.

Under Section 127 (3) a married person who runs away with a lover is caught by the law.

Under sub-sections (1) and (2) it is the third party who is being punished for 'interfering' in a marriage. In sub-section (3) it is the married man or woman who is punished for acting in a way which is detrimental to his/her marriage.

What is elopement?

The offence has been defined in several cases.

CASE: *Uganda v Solomon and Another* [1971] EA 46 High Court of Uganda

The first respondent (a man) was charged with eloping with a married woman not his wife and the second respondent (a woman) was charged with eloping with a person who was not her husband. The magistrate acquitted the respondent on the ground that the acts constituting elopement are not defined in the Penal Code Act and that therefore the offence is not defined within Article 15(8) of the Constitution.

On revision it was **held**: 'The offence of elopement is defined in the Act, although there is no specific definition of the word "elope".'

Justice Goudie said:

Article 15(8) of the Constitution reads: 'No person shall be convicted of a criminal offence unless that offence is defined and the penalty therefore is prescribed in a written law.'[2]

The words 'prescribed' in a written law seem to me to govern the word 'penalty' and it is sufficient for the offence to be 'defined'.

I do not consider the word 'defined' necessarily means there must be a formal definition but that the dictionary definition of 'define' applies, 'to make definite in outline'.

Section 121 A reads as follows:
1. Any person who elopes with a married woman or entices or causes a married woman to elope with him commits an offence and shall be liable ...
2. Any person being a female, who elopes with a married man or entices or causes a married man to elope commits an offence ...

It seems to me that the offences under (1) and (2) are made sufficiently definite in outline to comply with the requirements of Article 15 (8) of the Constitution. It is true that the word 'elope' itself is not defined but neither is the word 'assault' under the various offences covered by sections 227-230 of the Penal Code.

Certain sections such as S.245 (Theft), 272 (Robbery), 288 (False Pretence), 280 (Breaking and Entering) have formal definitions of the particular offences and the marginal notes use the word 'definition'. It should, however, be noted that these are rather exceptions to the general practice throughout the Code of creating an offence by the mere use of the words 'Any person who ...'

A formal definition is given when one is considered necessary to explain the nature of the offence or a particular word or phrase but is omitted where the words themselves explain the offence. Thus, there are few definitions, as such, in the offences referred to in chapters VII and VIII and equally few in chapter IX ...

The offence created by S 121 A is to 'elope' with a married person. ... it is perfectly well understood by most people ... through historical connections as meaning 'running away with' – usually from some kind of home. The dictionary definition covers running away with an unmarried as well as a married woman but even this difficulty is covered by the section itself which restricts or 'defines' if one prefers the word, the offence as meaning only running away with married persons.

What has to be proved?

The prosecution in an elopement case has to prove:
1. That one or both of the parties was married and living with his/her husband/wife.
2. That the accused knew the marital situation.

Marital status of the accused's 'partner' is an ingredient which must be proved in a case of elopement

CASE: *Uganda v Francis Ogema* HC Cr Revision 436 of 1970

The two accused, a man and a woman, were charged with elopement contrary to Section 121A (1) and (2) of the Penal Code. They were both convicted. The charge sheet had one statement of offence and two sets of particulars one relating to the man and the other relating to the woman.

Held on revision:

1. There should have been two separate counts each with a statement of offence and particulars of the offence. The particulars of the offence relating to the man which alleged that Ogema 'being a married man eloped with Sophia not being your wife' were defective. The particulars of the offence under Section 121A (1) must state that the woman is married, otherwise no offence will be revealed against the male accused.

2. When the accused denies an offence, the prosecution must adduce evidence to prove every ingredient of the offence. In this case no evidence whatsoever was led by the prosecution to show that the male accused was a married man.

CASE: *Uganda v Dhafa Nakalyaku* (1971) HCB 190

A female accused was charged with eloping with a man who was not her husband. Justice Jones **held**:

> The charge against the woman was bad as she was charged with eloping with a married man, not her husband. Section 121 A (2) did not cover such a situation, and there was nothing anywhere on the record to hint or suggest that Accused 1 was a married man or if he were married that Accused 2 (the woman) knew that he was married.

CASE: *Uganda v Solomon and Another* [1971] EA 46 High Court of Uganda

The first respondent (a man) was charged with eloping with a married woman not his wife and the second respondent (a woman) was charged with eloping with a person who was not her husband.

On revision it was **held**:

> The charge against the second respondent was bad as it did not allege elopement with a married man.

> The charge against the second respondent is bad in law. The defect in the charge is that under S 121 A (2) it is necessary in order to constitute an offence that the woman elope 'with a married man'. In the particulars of the charge, it must be specified that the man with whom she is alleged to have eloped was in fact a married man.

CASE: *Uganda v Alipakusadi Waluwayo & Another* Crim Revision 227/1974

Chief Justice Wambuzi said:

> The accused a man and a woman were charged with elopement contrary to Section 121A (1) and (2) of the Penal Code. The facts of the case were that on the relevant day the complainant left his wife at home and went to work. On his return he found his wife absent. The complainant made a report to the authorities. Later the woman was found at the home of A1 and both A1 and A2 were arrested.

Each was convicted on own plea of guilty. A1 had pleaded thus: 'I did elope with Abisaji'. A2 said: 'I did elope with Alipakusadi.'

Held:

1. For an offence to be committed under Section 121 (2) a woman must elope with a married man. The particulars did not allege that A1 was a married man.
2. The plea on each count was not unequivocal. The man did not admit that the woman with whom he eloped was a married woman and the woman did not admit that the man with whom she eloped was a married man.
3. It would be rash to conclude that merely because A2 was missing from her home and was found on the same day at A1's home that A2 must have eloped with A1.

Sentence set aside and if fine and compensation paid to be refunded.

Impossible to elope with spouse who has left her/his matrimonial abode permanently

Can the offence of elopement be committed if the woman is separated from her husband?

In *Uganda v Solomon and Another* [1971] EA 46 *Uganda v Ojok and Another* [1973] EA 489. High Court it was stated that:

> There is no very clear answer but probably, if the separation was intended to be a permanent one no complaint would be made. So the question would never arise. If it did arise the magistrate might refuse to convict for lack of *mens rea*. If he decided to convict he might take the view that the separated spouse was not an 'aggrieved person' and refuse compensation. In any event, 'hard cases make bad law'.

CASE: *Uganda v Olungu* [1972] EA 136 High Court of Uganda

The complainant was lawfully married to one Petofina. Evidence available showed that the woman (Petofina) left the complainant's home 4 years prior to the alleged elopement and had refused to return to him. The wife's father testified that she had lived with him for 5 years before marrying the accused. The accused was nevertheless convicted of elopement. On revision:

On revision, Rusell Ag.J said *inter alia* that:

> The word elopement implies running away with – usually from some kind of home. In this case the wife had run away from her husband at least 4 years prior to the alleged offence and it appears to me obvious that once she had permanently left the matrimonial abode the accused could not have committed elopement.

Held: that it is impossible to elope with a woman who has already left her husband.

CASE: *Uganda v Ojok and Another* [1973] EA 489 High Court

The accused were convicted of elopement. The woman was not living with her husband at the time of the alleged offence, having left him sometime before. The bride price had not been returned to her husband but the woman had moved in with her uncle. The man was ordered to pay compensation to the woman's father. Count 2 was as follows: A2 Rose at Alielo village eloped with Peter Ojok who is not her husband.

On revision it was **held:**
1. The count against the woman was bad in law as it did not allege that the man was married. The conviction cannot be supported.
2. It is impossible to elope with a woman who has already left her husband.
3. The aggrieved person to whom compensation can be ordered is only the spouse.

Saied also noted that since the woman had left her matrimonial abode permanently, this would negate any *mens rea* in so far as the male accused was concerned. The fact that dowry had not been refunded did not in the judge's opinion, affect the situation in any way. Permanent departure from the matrimonial abode by the female accused negatives *mens rea* of the offence

Knowledge of the other party's marital status is relevant for a conviction
CASE: *Uganda v Damulira* [1976] HCB 11 High Court
The two accused persons were charged with elopement under Sections 121 A (1) and (3). The second accused a married woman had run away from her husband and after 10 months she was found and arrested in a house used by the first accused as a shop. She denied having lived with the first accused as husband and wife.

Held: In order to prove elopement it must be shown that in case of a married woman the man charged had the necessary intention to make her abandon her husband and live with him as husband and wife. He must therefore know that at the time he took her away she was in fact married to another man and that the marriage has not been legally dissolved.

CASE: *Uganda v Solomon and Another* [1971] EA 46
The issue was whether the 'intention' must be shown in order to convict.

On revision court held *inter alia* that unless the contrary is shown, some degree of *mens rea* is implied in all offences.

> If the accused could show sufficient evidence to raise a reasonable doubt that he had grounds for believing that the person with whom he eloped was married, this would in my view, probably be a good defence but this would be difficult if he knew her surname or the matrimonial abode or even if he did not bother to enquire her matrimonial status.

What constitutes knowledge?
CASE: *Uganda v Rukwandura* [1973] EA 574. High Court of Uganda.
Two people, a man and a woman were prosecuted for elopement. Each was charged in individual counts with the offence under Section 121 A Penal Code Act. The male under 121 A (1) and the female under subsection 2.

Against the man it was alleged that he eloped with 'a married woman not being his wife under the custody of her husband'. The man's defence was that before he married the second accused, he approached her sister to ascertain her marital status. It was only after he had been told that she was not married that he took her for his wife. He paid the sister some money, probably by way of brideprice.

In convicting the accused persons, the trial magistrate said: 'The mere fact that the accused did not know that the woman was married is not an excuse. He should have taken the initiative to ascertain the situation as the woman has a child.'

The High Court **held** that knowledge that the other party is married is an essential of the offence of elopement.

Judgement:

It is now well settled, that the *mens rea* is just as much an ingredient of the offence of elopement as it is of the offence of adultery under S. 150 A. This means that it is a defence to the offence of elopement if the offender genuinely believes on reasonable grounds that the person with whom he or she elopes is not married. ... It would be competent for an accused person charged with having committed elopement, to show by evidence that in fact at the time of the elopement, he did not know that the woman was married to any person. But as pointed out in *Uganda v Solomon*, 'this would be difficult if he knew her surname or the matrimonial abode or even if he did not bother to inquire her marital status.'

And as expounded in *Uganda v Wodada* '... wilful blindness to the married state of the woman would be no defence if, on the facts, the court is able to hold that it was equivalent to actual knowledge. If a man suspects that a woman is married and realises its probability, but refrains from obtaining the final confirmation because he wanted in the event to deny knowledge, this is wilful blindness which would not afford a defence.'

... The fact that a woman has a child does raise a strong presumption that she might be married but it is a rebuttable presumption of fact. What is required is a final confirmation of the woman's marital status and notwithstanding the fact that the woman had a child; her sister provided that final confirmation. This added to the woman's evidence that she had divorced her husband adequately rebutted any presumption which might have arisen on account of the child. There was thus ample evidence which cast serious doubts regarding *mens rea*.

Result: The sentence against the man was quashed. Nor should the woman have been convicted, for it is clear that under Section 121A (2), a female only commits an offence if she elopes with a married man. The particulars in count 2 were defective in omitting to state this fact.

Who is an aggrieved party?

As seen in the Section creating the offence of elopement, a person (A) convicted for running away with a married person (B) can in addition to a sentence of imprisonment or a fine, be required to pay compensation to B's spouse. I presume that the compensation goes to B's spouse because A has interfered with the right of B's spouse to enjoy B's company. This provision is in line with the law on consortium within marriage law. The marriage relationship imposes certain legal duties on each partner or spouse and gives to each spouse rights arising out of marriage. At common law, the said rights are described as consortium. These include the right to companionship, comfort, company, sexual intercourse and cooperation. It is presumably on the basis of the right to consortium that a person who elopes with a married person is required to compensate the aggrieved party for loss of companionship at the very least.

It is however noted that unlike the criminal law of adultery, the criminal law on elopement does not differentiate between male and female offenders and cannot be criticised for being discriminatory against women.

In *Uganda v Ojok and Another* [1973] EA 489, Uganda's High Court clearly stated that in elopement, it is only a spouse who can be an aggrieved party. The father of a married woman with whom an accused man has eloped cannot be compensated as an aggrieved party.

CASE: *Uganda v Francis Ogema* HC Cr Revision 436 of 1970
- An aggrieved party for purposes of section 121A means the husband of the woman with whom the accused elopes under sub-section (1) or the wife of the man with whom the accused elopes under sub-section (2).
- The court is not entitled to assume that the husband or wife of a spouse who has eloped is an aggrieved party unless such a party says so.
- An order for compensation under the section is not automatic unless it has been shown that there is an aggrieved party, but if a party shows that he has been aggrieved by the offence, then it becomes mandatory for the court to make an order for compensation.

Court has no power to order woman to go back to her husband
CASE: *Uganda v Akua and Another* [1973] EA 246 High Court
The appellants were convicted of elopement and the man was ordered to pay compensation, the magistrate at the same time making an order for the attachment of his property. The woman was ordered to return to her husband.
On revision it was held:
- The court has no power to order a woman to return to her husband. The court cannot force a wife to live with her husband.
- No order for compensation should be made unless the spouse is shown to be aggrieved by the elopement.
Wambuzi said *inter alia*:

> The term 'aggrieved' is not defined in the Section. There can be no doubt that elopement is a criminal offence and a charge therefore is instituted in the name of the state. It appears that the offence is committed under the section, whether or not the husband of the woman with whom the accused elopes knows about it and indeed under Section 121 A (2) whether or not the wife of the man with whom the accused elopes knows about it.

> Who then is the aggrieved party?

> The husband of the woman with whom the accused elopes under sub-section (1) or the wife of the man with whom the accused elopes under sub-section (2). However the court is not entitled to assume that a party is aggrieved unless such party says so. In the instant case the husband of the woman complained to court. The order made by the magistrate should have been to pay the relevant compensation to the woman's husband. On the other hand there was no evidence that the male accused was a married man. The order made by the magistrate for the accused woman to pay compensation was misconceived.

> It appears that an order for compensation is not automatic unless it has been shown that there is an aggrieved party. In other words, if a party shows that he has been aggrieved by the commission of the offence, then it becomes mandatory for the court to make an order for compensation. The court cannot make an order in a vacuum.

Where there is an aggrieved party compensation is mandatory

CASE: *Uganda v Kezekiya Katigo and Another* Crim Revision 313/1974. High Court
The complainant and A2 got married and lived together for 12 years after which A1
eloped with A2. A1 and A2 were charged and convicted. A1 was sentened to 6 months
imprisonent and he also paid compensation to the complainant. A1 was later released
and he again eloped with A2. A1 was then charged with elopement, the subject of this
case.

Court noted that even when A1 was in prison, A2 was staying in A1's home until he
was released. The complainant was aware of the fact that his wife (A2) was staying
in the 'prisoner's' home but did not take any action until A1 was released. It was also
realised on trial that A1 was not a married man so as to bring 121 A (2) into application
and thus the prosecution withdrew the charges against the woman (A2).

The court went ahead to convict A1 but refused to make an order for compensation.
The magistrate's refusal was based on the 'fact that the complainant, husband of the
woman with whom A1 eloped appeared to be intending to use the elopement as a
trade. He took no action regarding the fact that his wife was living in the house of the
prisoner. He should seek remedy from the civil courts.'

On revision, the following issues were raised:

1. Whether there could be conviction where the woman was not cohabiting with
   her husband at the material time.
2. Whether the court had discretion to grant compensation to an aggrieved party.

Held:

1. Elopement under 121 A (1) and 121 A (2) could only be committed when the
   married party was cohabiting with her or his spouse or when that married party
   was living in the matrimonial home.
2. In the instant case A2 was not cohabiting with her husband, the complainant
   when A1 was arrested and charged with elopement. Therefore A1 committed
   no offence of elopement.
3. Section 121A (1) provided: 'Any person who elopes with a married woman or
   causes a married woman to elope with him, commits an offence' The word
   'entices' in the section had to be read with the phrase ' ... to elope with him' in
   the section. Similarly the married woman enticed to elope had to be cohabiting
   with her husband for it was only then that there could be elopement. A1 therefore
   did not commit the offence of enticing A2 to elope with him from the complainant.
4. The phrase 'the court shall order' made it mandatory on the court to order payment
   of compensation. The court had only discretion regarding the amount of
   compensation payable on subsequent conviction up to a maximum of Shs 1,200.

Conclusion on legal requirements for compensation

1. The 'aggrieved' party has been interpreted to be limited to 'the spouse of a
   person whose wife or husband has eloped'.
2. Compensation will only be paid to a husband/wife if he/she has complained about
   the elopement. This would be evidence that such a husband/wife is aggrieved.
3. Where there is an aggrieved spouse compensation is mandatory.

1. Originally Section 134 B.
2. Originally Section 134 A.
3. Originally Section 131.
4. Originally Section 121A.
5. At the time of the case in question, the 1967 Constitution was the relevant constitution. I however note that an almost identical provision exists in the 1995 constitution. In its Article 28 (12) it is provided that except for contempt of court, no person shall be convicted of a criminal offence unless the offence is defined and the penalty for it prescribed by law.

11

Bigamy:
Section 153 of the Uganda Penal Code Act.[1]

Section 153:

> Any person who, haing a husband or wife living, goes through a ceremony of marriage which is void by reason of its taking place during the life of such a husband or wife commits a felony and is liable to imprisonment for five years; except that this Section shall not extend to any person whose marriage with such husband or wife has been declared void by a court of competent jurisdiction, nor to any person who contracts a marriage during the life of a former husband or wife, if such husband or wife, at the time of the subsequent marriage, shall have been continually absent from such person for the space of seven years, and shall not have been heard of by such person as being alive within that time.

When a married person goes through a ceremony of marriage with a third party, knowing that his/her spouse is still alive, such a person will have committed bigamy. Thus if A who is married to B goes through a marriage ceremony with C, A would have committed bigamy if he/she is aware that B is still alive and that the marriage to the first partner (B) is still valid.

The justification for making bigamy an offence is that it endangers the sanctity of marriage by profaning the ceremony.

Proofs and defences

Under Section 153, where the first marriage has been declared void by a court of competent jurisdiction then the second marriage ceremony will not amount to bigamy.

The section further states that where a person (A) contracts a marriage during the life of her/his spouse (B), such would not be bigamy if the spouse (B) has, at the time of the subsequent marriage, been continually absent from such person (A) for at least 7 years and (A) has not heard of (B) being alive within that period. This is a complete defence.

The accused can also adduce evidence that at the time of the second marriage, he/she believed on reasonable grounds that his or her spouse was dead, although there has not been absence for 7 years.

It is reported by Card, Cross and Jones[2] that the prosecution must prove that the accused went through a valid marriage ceremony with the 'first' spouse. This can be done through production of a marriage certificate or the calling of witnesses who were present at the first ceremony to identify the parties.

According to Card, Cross and Jones, once the parties are proved to have gone through a ceremony of marriage, there is a rebuttable presumption of law that it is valid.

The prosecution must also prove that the first spouse is alive.

The offence of bigamy is not committed by one who honestly and reasonably, albeit mistakenly, believes the former spouse to be dead. See *Reg v King* [1964] 1 QB 285; *Reg v Gould* [1968] 2 Q.B 65.

Bigamy versus polygamy

Uganda's law recognises polygamous unions as valid marriages. Both customary marriages and marriages according to Islam are potentially polygamous. Thus, when a man contracts a potentially polygamous marriage, his subsequent marriage to another woman during the subsistence of the first marriage, would not constitute bigamy. I however note that in Uganda, men sometimes contract monogamous marriages, e.g. church marriages and civil marriages and during the subsistence of such marriages they thereafter go through customary marriage ceremonies with parties other than their first wives. By entering monogamous marriages with their first partners, such men would have lost their 'right' to be polygamous. Consequently the second marriage ceremonies in which they purport to marry subsequent wives constitute an offence: bigamy.

---

1. Originally section 150.
2. Criminal Law, 12th Edition (1992), page 437.

12

Incest:
Sections 149-151 of the Uganda Penal Code Act.[1]

Section 149

(1) Any person who has sexual intercourse with another person with whom, to his knowledge, any of the following relationships exists

Mother	Father
Mother's daughter	Father's son
Daughter	Son
Father's mother	Mother's father
Mother's mother	Father's father
Son's daughter	Son's son
Daughter's daughter	Daughter's son
Sister	Brother
Wife's mother	Husband's father
Wife's daughter	Husband's son
Father's sister	Father's brother
Mother's sister	Mother's brother
Brother's daughter	Brother's son
Sister's daughter	Sister's son
Father's brother's daughter	Father's brother's son
Mother's sister's daughter	Mother's sister's son
Son's wife	Daughter's husband
Father's wife	Mother's husband

commits on offence and is liable to imprisonment for seven years or, if that other person is under the age of eighteen years of age, to imprisonment for life.

(2) It is immaterial that sexual intercourse took place with the consent of the other person.

The offence of incest is aimed at preventing sexual intercourse between people of specified relationships, persons within certain specified degrees of consanguinity. In general, the relationships are blood relationships. As is the case with most other sexual offences, it does not apply to sexual acts short of penetrative sex/sexual intercourse.

Prior to the 1990 amendment to the Code, Uganda's law had adopted the western concept of incest and thus prohibited sexual relationships within the nuclear family: brother-sister, father-daughter, mother-son, grandparent-grandchild. The 1990 amendment widened the types of relationships within which sexual intercourse is prohibited. Whereas some of the new relationships are based on blood relationships, some other 'familial' relationships were criminalised.

It is noted that incest is also handled under the laws on marriage. For example, under the Customary Marriage (Registration) At Chapter 248, *Laws of Uganda*, Revised Edition, 2000 marriage between persons with specified relationships is prohibited. It is noted that the relationships on which criminal prosecution can be based in case of sexual intercourse are identical to the relationships which the Marriage Act refers to as 'Prohibited Degrees of Kinship' for purposes of marriage.

Whereas some of the newly prohibited relationships conform to what some communities in Uganda in fact prohibit, they may be contrary to the culturally sanctioned behaviour of others. Perhaps in a culturally heterogeneous society as is the Ugandan society it is not surprising that what may be acceptable to one community is taboo to another. Nevertheless since culture is not a defence to a criminal charge it is what is provided for in the penal law that prevails against culture.

The purpose of the law of incest

In as far as the relationships based on blood are concerned; one can safely say that the major purpose was to prevent any genetic risks which may attach to conception. The law is perhaps also aimed at protecting the young and the vulnerable within the institution of the family. This would be true of blood as well as non-blood relationships. It can also be safely contended that the law of incest is in the main a reproduction of social cultural norms and values about sex and sexuality. In as far as close blood relationships are concerned criminal incest also conforms to some Biblical as well as Islamic principles.

It must be noted that consent between the parties to have sexual intercourse is not a defence to the charge (Section 149 (2)). Further more, the law criminalises the act even where the two people involved are both adults. Note that when one of the parties to the incestuous sexual act is under the age of 18 years, the adult person is liable to a harsher punishment (Section 149 (1)).

Consent of the DPP to prosecution
Section 151

> No prosecution for an offence under Section 149 shall be commenced without the sanction of the Director of Public Prosecutions.

Incest is one of the few offences which require the sanction of the Director of Public Prosecutions before parties can be prosecuted. A court thus has no power to hear the case unless the prosecution has produced a letter from the relevant office indicating that the DPP has given his consent to the proceedings.

Proof

What is important for the prosecution to prove against an accused are the following ingredients:
- That sexual intercourse took place
- That the parties fall within one of the prohibited relationships
- That the party had knowledge that his/her sexual partner was 'related' to him or her

It therefore follows that lack of knowledge that one's sexual partner is a relative is a defence.

Section 150: Test of relationship

In section 149, the expressions 'brother' and 'sister' respectively include half-brother and half sister, and the section shall apply whether the relationship between the person charged with an offence and the person with whom the offence is alleged to have been committed is or is not traced through lawful wedlock.Section 150 provides that the law covers any of the relevant relationship, even when this is not the result of a lawful marriage. What is thus important is that there is a blood relationship.

Under Section 150 the code specifically provides that the law of incest covers the relationships of half brothers and half sisters. What therefore is crucial is that the parties share at least one parent.

The relationship need not be traced through lawful wedlock

CASE: *Barugahara v Uganda* [1969] EA 73 High Court

The appellant was convicted of incest with his daughter under Section 144(1) of the Penal Code Act. He had lived with a woman 17 years before the alleged offence but they never married. The woman left his home while pregnant. When his daughter was 12 years old she came to live with him. The daughter became pregnant.

Held:

- The offence of incest is committed even if the relationship is not traced through lawful wedlock.
- The evidence of a female witness (here the daughter) liable to be prosecuted for incest requires to be corroborated.

This holding is in line with the need for corroboration in sexual offences. The important point in *Barugahara* was that the accused had had sexual intercourse with his biological daughter. The fact that the girl's mother and father had never been married was irrelevant.

Adoptive relationships

According to Card, Cross and Jones (1992:242) and according to L.B.Curzon (1997:208), in England, incest does not apply to adoptive relationships. The Uganda Penal Code is silent on this point and the issue has never been brought before a court of law. In its report on a *Study on Rape, Defilement and other Sexual offences*, the Uganda Law Reform Commission recommended that since an adopted child is treated as a natural child of the offender in other areas of the law (e.g. inheritance), it should be deemed an offence to have sexual intercourse with the adopted person. If we agree that one of the purposes of the law on incest is to protect sexual exploitation of vulnerable members of the family, I would argue that the law be extended to adoptive relationships.

---

[1] Originally section 144.

13

Prostitution and related Offences:
Sections 136-139 of the Uganda Penal Code Act

Before the 1990 amendment to the Penal Code, prostitution was not an offence although related acts such as soliciting for customers in a public place, living on earnings of prostitution as well as running brothels were all punishable under the law. What the law did then was to make prostitution difficult but not impossible. It has been argued by many that prostitution has social value and that it is for this reason that in many jurisdictions, prostitution is tolerated as it was in Uganda before 1990. One of the most common reasons given is that it is a safety valve for male sexuality which is uncontrollable. It is contended that men who are away from their wives would in the absence of prostitutes be 'forced' into other vices such as rape and homosexuality.

If indeed Ugandan society believed that prostitution has social value, the AIDS pandemic changed its views and as a result prostitution in itself was criminalised by the 1990 amendment to the penal Code.

Under Section 139[1] the 1990 Statute created the offence of prostitution and any person who engages or practises prostitution is guilty of an offence.

Section 138[2] defines prostitution. The following points are worth taking note of:
- The offence can be committed by both men and women.
- The essence of prostitution is that a person *offers* herself or himself to avail sexual services to others for consideration/payment.
- The payment may be in terms of money or other material gain.
- The sexual activity may be sexual intercourse or any other sexual act.
- The conduct in question will be criminal whether it takes place in public or in private.
- In addition to creating the new offence of prostitution the 1990 Statute raised the punishments to which an accused can be sentenced for offences related to prostitution.

Section 139 provides that:

Any person who practises or engages in prostitution commits an offence and is liable to imprisonment for seven years.

The sexual activity may be sexual intercourse or any other sexual act

The law does not limit itself to sexual intercourse, i.e. penetration of the female organ by the male organ. It covers sexual conduct such as homosexuality (sodomy) as well as non-penetrative sexual acts such as masturbation. What is essential is that the sexual activity has been paid for.

Does the section catch the customer?

A look at Section 138 indicates that a prostitute is the person who receives 'consideration', who is paid/earns from the transaction and not the person who makes the payment. Although I have not come across any judicial decision dealing with the criminal responsibility of the customer, I opine that using section 19(1) (c) and of (b) of the Penal Code Act, a customer is as guilty of prostitution as is the `prostitute'.

Section 19 is entitled 'Principal offenders' and provides 19 (1)

> When an offence is committed, each of the following persons is deemed to have taken part in committing the offence and to be guilty of the offence and may be charged with actually committing it
>
> (a) every person who aids or abets another person in committing the offence.
>
> (b) every person who does or omits to do any act for the purpose of enabling or aiding another person to commit the offence.

Since the customer enables the prostitute to engage in the illegal act, the customer should be treated as a principal offender.

The offence can be committed by both men and women
This interpretation is based on the fact that the section refers to a person who holds *himself* or *herself* out as available.

But despite the gender neutral language of the section, prostitution can be looked at as a sex specific offence on the basis that agents of the criminal justice system (e.g. the Police) are more likely to arrest women found 'loitering' in public places than they are to arrest men.

Offering ones self as available
The section does not require that an accused be arrested in an act of sexual intercourse. It is not necessary that there be evidence that the accused in fact engaged in a sexual act. What is important/essential is that the accused's conduct can be interpreted beyond reasonable doubt to indicate that he/she was willing/available for sexual gratification in exchange for gain. One can thus conclude that any attempt to get a customer is in itself a crime, just as much as engaging in a sexual act for monetary or other gain.

To prove *beyond reasonable doubt* that the particular conduct of an individual can be interpreted as making one's self-available for sexual gratification for gain is not easy. And it is for this reason that women who are arrested in public places and whose conduct could on a balance of probabilities be interpreted as prostitution are often charged under Section 167 of the Penal Code rather than under Sections 138 and 139.

Section 167:

> Any person who (e) without lawful excuse, publicly does any indecent act.
>
> (f) in any public place solicits or loiters for immoral purposes; shall be deemed an idle and disorderly person.

Living on earnings of prostitution: Section 136[3]
Section 136 (1) creates two separate offences:
1. Living on earnings of prostitution and
2. Soliciting or importuning for immoral purposes

It provides thus:

> Every person who knowingly lives wholly or in part on the earnings of prostitution and every person who in any place solicits or importunes for immoral purposes commits an offence and is liable to imprisonment for seven years.

Under Section 136 it is an offence to live on the earnings of prostitution. This section covers persons who act as commercial agents for the prostitutes, for example pimps, but does not catch the prostitute.

Under **Section 136 (2)** the law shifts the evidential burden of proving that one is knowingly living on earnings of prostitution to an accused. It provides as follows:

> Whether a person is proved to live with or to be habitually in the company of a prostitute or is proved to have exercised control, direction or influence over the movements of a prostitute in such a manner as to show that he or she is aiding, abetting or compelling his or her prostitution with any other person, or generally, that person shall, unless he or she shall satisfy the court to the contrary, be deemed to be knowingly living on the earnings of prostitution.

The effect of section 136(2) is that if the prosecution is to establish that a particular accused person is guilty of knowingly living on earnings of prostitution, all it has to prove is that the accused is:

1. living with a prostitute or
2. habitually in the company of a prostitute or
3. exercising control, direction or influence over the movements of a prostitute.

Once the prosecution proves any of the above, the case will have been proved against the accused under section 136(1). It is only if the accused satisfies the court to the contrary i.e. introduces evidence to disapprove the allegation (on a balance of probabilities) that he/she is knowingly living on the earnings of the prostitute that such accused will escape conviction.

CASE: *Shaw v DPP* [1962] AC 220 House of Lords

The appellant (Shaw) published a booklet, The Ladies' Directory, of some 28 pages. Most of the pages were taken up with the names and addresses of prostitutes. The matter published left no doubt that the advertisers (the prostitutes) could be got in touch with at the telephone numbers given and were offering their services for sexual intercourse and in some cases, for the practice of sexual perversions. The appellant's avowed purpose in publication was to assist prostitutes to carry on their trade because the law did not allow them to solicit in the street. The prostitutes paid for the advertisements and the appellant derived a profit from the publication. Among other things, Shaw was charged with and convicted of living on the earnings of prostitution. Shaw appealed to the House of Lords

The appellant argued that the trial judge had misdirected the jury in that he had failed to point out the distinction between services supplied to a prostitute for reward and the mere receipt of the earnings of a prostitute, and that the appellant had not received the earnings of prostitutes, but profits from the sale of the booklet, after all expenses had been met. It was further submitted that there was no evidence that the appellant charged inflated prices for the prostitutes' advertisement. Counsel for the appellant also pointed out the fact that the magazine also contained advertisements for models and clubs.

Held *inter alia* by the House of Lords that a person might fairly be said to be living in whole or in part on the earnings of prostitution if he was paid by prostitutes for goods or services supplied by him to them.

Judgement:

In our view, the principle of Thomas' case is equally applicable in a case such as the one now before us. *If a man knowingly assists a prostitute with the direct object of enabling her to carry on her trade and knowingly lives wholly or in part on the earnings of the prostitution, which he assists, he is guilty of the offence.*

It was further submitted that there was no evidence that the appellant charged inflated prices for the prostitute's advertisements and that Thomas' case was distinguished.

This submission involves a misunderstanding of the relevance of the inflated rent in that case. The purpose of tendering evidence as to the rent was to show that the room was not let for normal accommodation but for the prostitutes' professional purposes.

Would the decision in the presence case cover the caser of a doctor or lawyer giving their services to a prostitute and receiving from her payment for such services?

The House of Lords answered thus:

'The landlords and estate agents in letting flats and providing flats for individual prostitutes are in so doing engaged in the occupation of landlords and estate agents and were plainly living on their own earnings and not on those of the prostitutes. The test is whether the man is doing an honest job of work and not work which by its nature is parasitic on the earnings of the prostitute. In the present case, the appellant received payments out of the moneys earned by the prostitutes, not in pursuance of a real occupation as a publisher rendering his professional services but by preying as a parasite or hanger-on, and in that sense living on these prostitutes in order to take moneys from them. If he lived even partly on their earnings, it is sufficient, even if he did not live wholly on such earnings.

'When a prostitute pays money for goods received and services rendered, and pays the market rate for the good and fair rate for the services, she has had the benefit of her earning and no other persons can be said to have the benefit of those earnings. If, however, she pays an excessive price for those goods and services, then as to the extent of the excess, it may be said that another has the benefit of the prostitutes' earnings.

'In this case the services rendered by the appellant are directly promoting the prostitution and to as great an extent as if done by a procurer. Equally there must be services rendered to a prostitute which are not rendered to her qua prostitute, for example, the baker who sells bread, the physician who attends to her, the barrister who represents her in court.

'The exorbitance of the charge made to the prostitute is relevant in two ways:

'(1) to establish the knowledge of the accused that he is living on the earnings of prostitution.(2) to establish the purpose for which the service is rendered. If an exorbitant rent is charged for a flat, that is some evidence that the landlord knows that *the lessee is a prostitute* and that he knows the purpose for which the flat is let. It was said that there was no evidence that an excessive charge was made to the prostitutes in respect of their advertisements. This is quite irrelevant where the service is, as here, unequivocally for the purposes of promoting prostitution. Further, it matters not whether it is the prostitute who pays or some other person provided that the payment has been earned by reason of prostitution. For example, the doorman at the brothel who receives tips from the clients. If the purpose for which the gods supplied or the services rendered is directly concerned with the prostitution, that is, for the purpose of promoting it, then an offence has been committed, but not if those goods are supplied, or the services rendered to the prostitutes qua human being. As regards a publication consisting of advertisements of models, photographers and prostitutes, in so far as it related to advertisements from prostitutes the publisher would be living partly on the earnings of prostitution. If a service is rendered to the prostitute as an ordinary member of the public, then the accused cannot be said to be knowingly living on the earnings of prostitution.

' A landlord who lets a whole block of flats to a prostitute at the normal market rent is not living on the prostitute. However, a wholly extortionate rent or charge of any kind demanded of a pro ·'tute may be evidence to show that the male person is living parasitically on the ea. ·s of prostitution in relation to such extortionate rent or charge as is demanded.'

CASE: *Karuria v Republic* [1969] EA 16
The appellant was a prostitute living on her own earnings and was convicted on a charge of knowingly living on the earnings of a prostitute contrary to section 154 of the Kenyan Penal Code (identical to Section 136 of the Ugandan Penal Code).
Held *inter alia* that the section does not intend to make every prostitute living on her own earnings guilty of an offence within the section. It is focused on punishing people other than the prostitute, who live on her earnings of prostitution.

Soliciting or importuning for immoral purposes
Even before prostitution was criminalised by the Penal Code Act, soliciting for clients in a public place was an offence. The reason for punishing such conduct was because society considered it an activity which was offensive to public order and decency.

Section 137: Brothels
Statute 4 of 1990 retained the offence of keeping a brothel. However the sentence for the offence was raised to imprisonment for seven years. The section provides that:

> Any person who keeps a house, room, set of rooms or place of any kind for purposes of prostitution commits an offence and is liable to imprisonment for seven years.

The purpose of the law in section 137 is to make prostitution difficult. The law prohibits the keeping of a brothel because it provides a place/premises for the prostitute to carry out his/her business. Although the Uganda Code does not define what a brothel is, it can be safely stated that these are premises, which are commercially availed to persons who are desirous of engaging in prostitution.

---

1. Originally Section 134 B
2. Originally Section 134 A.
3. Originally Section 131.

14

Unnatural Offences:
Section 145 of the Uganda Penal Code Act[1]

Unnatural offences are referred to as buggery at common law and although the term 'unnatural' offences is rather ambiguous, the provision is used to criminalise sodomy. **Section 145** provides that:

> Any person who:
> a) has carnal knowledge of any person against the order of nature;
> b) has carnal knowledge of an animal
> c) permits a male person to have carnal knowledge of him or her against the order of nature, commits an offence and is liable to imprisonment for life.

Section 145 (b) criminalises bestiality (having sexual intercourse with an animal). It covers intercourse *per anum* or *per vaginam* by a man or a woman with an animal. Sections 145(a) and (c) make anal sex between males as well as anal sex between a male and a female criminal. It thus prohibits homosexuality. According to Smith and Hogan (1992:476), buggery at common law consists in intercourse *per anum* by a man with a man, *per anum* by a man with a woman. The use of phrase 'carnal knowledge' in both subsections necessitates that there be penetration by a male organ. It is for this reason that where A (a male) penetrates the anus of B (another male), A will be prosecuted under Section.145 (a) and B would be prosecuted under Section 145 (c). Even where A (a male) penetrates the anus of C (a female), A would be prosecuted under Section145 (a) and C would be prosecuted under Section145 (c). According to Smith and Hogan (1992:477), the person effecting the intercourse is known as the agent and the other party as the patient.

As in rape, penetration must be proved if bestiality or a conviction under Section 145 (a) or (c) is to be entered.

Through Section 145 it is clear that society considers heterosexuality as normalcy of sexual behaviour. The use of the phrase 'unnatural' offences also indicates that sodomy is considered a most reprehensible form of sexual activity.

Women who perform sexual acts on each other are not caught by the current law because they do not possess a sexual organ with which to penetrate each other. Thus penile penetration is the defining criterion for the offence.

It has been argued by some feminists that the non-criminalisation of lesbianism arose out of the fact that it was considered so offensive that it is not even taken cognizance of. It is further contended that in fact it is not so much lesbianism, as female sexuality that society denies.[2] However, it is also possible that society believed that only men engaged in same sex relationship. Queen Victoria of England is even quoted to have said 'ladies would never engage in such despicable acts.'[3]

In Uganda's criminal law, 'unnatural offences' constitute a felony and since 1990 conviction calls for a most serious punishment – liability to imprisonment for life.

It need also be noted that any attempt to commit any of the offences specified in Section 145 also makes one liable to imprisonment for seven years. (Section 146).

The law thus equates homosexuality with serious offences such as manslaughter (section 187 i.e. unlawfully causing the death of another person); attempt to commit rape (section 125); attempt to murder (section 204); killing an unborn child (212) etc. which also call for imprisonment for life.

Societal reasons for prohibiting homosexuality

Gay rights activists argue that the disrepute of male homosexuality in law is because of the low status that women have in society. According to this argument, men view themselves, and are viewed as subjects, as authentic persons, and women, their sexual intimates as objects. For a man to relate to another man sexually means that he must 'reduce' himself to the level of a woman, by becoming an object for another man. This is seen as abhorrent and inappropriate.[4]If this argument is true then one can take it further. It would follow that both men and women who have sexual intercourse with animals are punished because they reduce themselves to the level of beasts. Thereby they degrade the whole human race.

Another alleged justification for criminalising male homosexuality is that societal construction of sexuality negates any sexual activity that is 'non-productive'. It is for this reason therefore that homosexual men are penalised: they are penalised for the loss of the semen which holds the seed for reproduction.

Citing *Jellyman* (1838) 8 C&P 604, Smith and Hogan (1992:477) state that the offence can be committed by a husband with his wife. This view perhaps arises out of the fact that the section creating the offence does not use the word 'unlawful'. If this conclusion is correct a policy question arises: Is the legal notion of privacy, held sacred in marital relationships, discarded when it comes to consensual sodomy within marriage? Does the need to penalise the man for the loss of seed outweigh the need for the law not to enter people's bedrooms?

Homosexuality from a religious perspective

Whatever other reasons are given for the criminalisation of homosexual behaviour we cannot ignore the strong force of religion. In several 'offences against morality', more than in any other part of the criminal law, sin is often equated with immorality and with crime. Both Christianity and Islam condemn homosexuality. In 'Islamic perspective' Munir El-Kassem, a Western dentistry professor and chaplain for Muslim students was asked his position on homosexuality and he answered:

> Homosexuality, from an Islamic [perspective] is an aberration of human behaviour – it is not regarded as normal behaviour. The Koran condemned people who took it as a lifestyle at the time of the prophet Lut and we were told that God enforced severe punishment on those people because of such behaviour. Sexual activity is considered a means of propagating the human race within love and compassion between two individuals – male and female – not people of the same gender.[5]

And according to the Muslim Women's League (MWL) in its 'An Islamic Perspective on Sexuality' it is stated that:

> In Islam, sexuality is considered part of our identity as human beings. In His creation of humankind, God distinguished us from other animals by giving us reason and will such

that we can control behaviour that, in other species, is governed solely by instinct. So, although sexual relations ultimately can result in the reproduction and survival of the human race, an instinctual concept, our capacity for self-control allows us to regulate this behaviour.

In specific reference to homosexuality the paper states:

> Human beings are capable of many forms of sexual expression, orientation and identification. The existence of such variety again is not found in any other species and thus further demonstrates our uniqueness among God's creations. The potential for behavior, such as homosexuality, does not mean that its practice is lawful in the eyes of God ... Homosexuality is thus prohibited.[6]

Several verses in the Bible speak negatively about homosexuality and refer to the practice as sin, an abomination and a mark of depravity. One can even conclude that reference to sodomy as unnatural acts by the Penal Code derives from the language of the Bible.

In Genesis Chapter 19 God destroyed the cities of Sodom and Gomorrah whose inhabitants' prevailing sin was homosexuality. In Leviticus 18:22 it is stated: 'You shall not lie with a man as with a woman, it is an abomination.' And according to Leviticus 20: 13 'If a man lies with a male as with a woman, both of them have committed an abomination; they shall be put to death; their blood is upon them.' In Romans 1:26-27 homosexuality is given as an example of the kind of behaviour that is a result of the rejection of God and it is stated that 'For this reason God gave them over to degrading passions; for their women exchanged the natural function for that which is unnatural, and in the same way also the men abandoned the natural function of the woman and burned in their desire toward one another, men with men committing indecent acts ...'. It is also written in 1 Corinthians that homosexuals will not be allowed into the kingdom of heaven and in 1 Timothy 1:11 homosexuality is classified among activities that are considered ungodly and sinful, being placed alongside such sins as murdering one's parents, kidnapping, etc.

I should also mention that although some scholars argue otherwise,[7] in African society today many voices 'against' homosexuality argue that the practice is un-African and should thus not be recognised as a norm.

---

1. Originally Section 140.
2. See Geetanjali Gongoli (2004) 'The Regulation of Women's Sexuality Through Law: Civil and Criminal Laws.' p. 2 of 4. http://www.hsph.harvard.edu/Organizations/healthnet/SAsia/repro2/regulation-throu .... Accessed on 24-06-04
3. Joanna Watson (2002) 'Women's Sexuality: Then and Now.'http://www.cwrl.utexas.edu/-ulrich/femhist/sexuality.shtml. Accessed on 24-06-04.
4. See Geetanjali Gongoli (2004) 'The Regulation of Women's Sexuality Through Law: Civil and Criminal Laws.' p. 2 of 4. http://www.hsph.harvard.edu/Organizations/healthnet/SAsia/repro2/regulation-throu .... Accessed on 24-06-04

5. The UWO Gazette – Volume 96, Issue 27 at http://www.gazette.uwu.ca/2002/October/171/ campus-and- culture5.htm. Accessed on 25-06-2004. page 1 of 2.

6. http://www.zawaj.com/articles/sexuality-league.html. Accessed on 25-06-2004.

7. See e.g. Tamale Sylvia (2003) *Feminist Africa: Issue 2*, 2003; Murray S and Roscoe W (1998) *Boy-Wives and Female Husbands: Studies of African Homosexualities.* New York: St. Martin's Press. Mushanga M (1973) "The Nkole of Southwestern Uganda" in Molnos A ed. *Cultural Source Materials for Population Planning in East Africa: Beliefs and Practices.* Nairobi: East African Publishing House. Southwold M (1973) "The Baganda of Central Uganda" in Molnos A ed. *Cultural Source Materials for Population Planning in East Africa: Beliefs and Practices.* Nairobi: East African Publishing House.

Uganda Law Reform Commission Report

Introduction

As earlier stated, Statute 4 of 1990 led to changes in the law on sexual offences. In several instances, new offences were created and punishments for existing offences were raised. But since the amendment was passed, a lot of questions have been raised:

- Is the law serving its purpose of protecting vulnerable members of society?
- Is the law leading to justice?
- To what extent does this law represent the aspirations of society?

Calls for amendment of the substantive as well as procedural law regarding sexual offences have abounded.

In 1997, at the request of Government, the Uganda Law Reform Commission undertook a study on the law relating to sexual offences. The study involved field research in six districts in Uganda representing the four geographical regions of the country. Focus Group Discussions were conducted and key informants were interviewed. Case studies were carried out on a few victims of sexual offences, and with offenders and families of both victims and offenders in sexual assault cases. Prior to the field study, a National Consultative Workshop was held with the aim of securing consensus on the themes of the study. Following the field study, three regional workshops were conducted to disseminate the findings of the study and to seek views on draft recommendations for amendments to the law on sexual offences. The recommendations culminated into The Sexual Offences (Miscellaneous Amendments) Bill, 2000.

In this section I will discuss some of the recommendations contained in the Bill.

Recommendations on the Law of Rape

Definition of Rape

The law on rape has been criticised both for its narrow focus on vaginal penetration by the male organ, and for its failure to recognise that other forced sexual acts may have as serious an impact (e.g trauma) on the victim as vaginal penetration. In the proposed amendment, rape was redefined *inter alia* as follows:

- Any person who performs a sexual act on another person without that person's consent commits a felony known as rape.
- 'Sexual act' means penetration of the vagina, mouth, or anus, however slight of any person by a sexual organ or the use of any object or organ by a person on another person's sexual organ.

One important effect of the amendment would be that forced anal sex (e.g. acts of homosexuality) would be treated as rape. This would distinguish consensual homosexual acts from forced homosexual acts which are currently viewed as unnatural acts. Furthermore, forced oral sex would also be treated as rape. Further still, the forced penetration of another person's sexual organ with an object or part of the body other than the penis would also be covered by ths law.

Another effect of the proposed amendment is that both men and women can be victims as well as perpetrators of rape. This would arise partly out of the fact that a sexual act through use of an object, through use of an organ other than the penis, for example a finger, would constitute rape.

The aim of making the offence gender-neutral comes out even more clearly in the proposed Section 117(1) (c) where it is provided that' a person who performs a sexual act with the consent of another person when the consent has been obtained ... in the case of a woman, by personating her husband or *in the case of a man, by personating his wife*, commits a felony known as rape.' (My emphasis)

Thus a woman who 'tricks' a man into a sexual act while the man is operating under the mistaken belief that the woman is his wife would be guilty of rape in the same way as a man who misrepresents himself to a woman has her husband and has sexual intercourse with her.

The Punishment for Rape

It is proposed that the *maximum* sentence for rape should be reduced from the death penalty to life imprisonment.

Several reasons have been given for the need to reduce the penalty for rape but I will mention just a few.

1. The raising of the penalty for rape, and for defilement of females under the age 18 years from life imprisonment to the death penalty in 1990 automatically meant that it is only the High Court which has power to try both rape and defilement cases. This has led to a high increase of prisoners on remand since the High Court does not have enough judges to expeditiously handle the huge number of prosecutions for rape and defilement. This not only overstretches prison resources but is also a violation of the constitutional right to a speedy trial. Since offences for which life imprisonment is the maximum penalty can be tried by Chief Magistrates' Courts, which are more numerous than High Court Judges, the amendment would be of value.

2. It has also been argued that attachment of the death penalty to rape and defilement cases may in fact be leading to non-reporting of such cases. According to findings by the Law Reform Commission, victims fear the wrath of the accused's family if they report such a case since it attracts the death sentence.

3. Another argument often put forward by proponents of abolition of the death penalty for convictions of rape and defilement (also put forward by the Commission) is that no court has since 1990 ever sentenced an offender to death.

But although the Commission proposed a reduction in the sentence, it is noted that it recommended that in some cases the trial court should be divested of discretion in determining the specific sentence for a convict of rape or defilement. The proposed law provides that in some cases the court should be obliged to sentence an offender to the maximum sentence of imprisonment for life. The commission was of the view that where the rape or defilement is committed in aggravating circumstances, the offender must be sentenced to life imprisonment.

Thus the proposed law provides:

- Punishment for rape Section 118 (2): where the Court is satisfied that there were aggravating circumstances in the commission of the offence, the person *shall* be sentenced to imprisoned for life (Emphasis mine).
- Section 118 (3): Where an accused person commits rape in circumstances other than what is prescribed in subsection (2), the court may sentence the offender to imprisonment other than imprisonment for life.
- Section 118 (4): In determining whether or not there are aggravating factors, the court shall take into account but shall not be limited to the following:
- Whether or not the offender is infected with a sexually transmitted disease.
- Whether or not the offender is infected with the Human Immune Virus (HIV) or suffering from Acquired Immune Deficiency Syndrome (AIDS).
- The age of the person against whom the offence was committed; or
- The extent of harm caused to the person against whom the offence was committed.

Thus where the offender is infected with a sexually transmitted disease or HIV, where the victim (survivor) of the sexual assault is a very young child and where the sexual assault is accompanied by or results into grievous injuries/harm, the court *must* sentene the offender to life imprisonment.

Mandatory testing for sexually transmitted diseases

The 1990 amendment to the Penal Code was strongly influenced by the AIDS pandemic in Uganda. And it is within the said context that women's rights activists called for harsher punishments for sexual offences. It was argued by many that an HIV positive person who forces another into a sexual act, or who engages in sexual activity with an underage girl and thus exposes the 'victim' to the risk of infection, is as culpable as a murderer. It was argued that both categories of people deserve the death penalty.

While debating the desirability of reducing the maximum penalty for rape and defilement, once again, the fear of HIV infection appears to be at the forefront of the minds of many people. It is thus no surprise that it is considered that somebody's HIV status should be relevant in determining the sentence to be given to a sexual offender. In the proposed law therefore, it is suggested that where the offender is HIV positive, that fact should be considered as an aggravating factor which should be taken into consideration in determining the sentence.

Thus under the proposed **Section 118 (5)**:

Mandatory testing for sexually transmitted diseases or HIV/AIDS shall by order of the court be carried out on the person convicted of rape unless there is other evidence proving that person to be suffering from AIDS.

According to this proposed law, once a person is convicted of rape, that person must be tested for sexually transmitted diseases and HIV/AIDS before the court determines the sentence.

Marital rape

Arguments for the abolition of the defence of existence of a marital relationship between the offender and the victim of a rape have already been presented in the discussion of the meaning of 'unlawful' sexual intercourse.

The commission reported that its findings revealed that sexual intercourse by a husband without the consent of the wife does occur. It was also noted that the law, custom and religion all stress the *right* of the husband to sexual intercourse within marriage.

In the proposed amendment it is provided that a married person who performs a sexual act with his or her spouse without the consent of that spouse, whether the spouses are living together or are separated, commits an offence known as 'marital sexual assault'. (Section 118 (A) (1)).

The effect of the proposed provision is to abolish the *absolute* right of a husband to sexual intercourse with his wife.

However, the proposed law treats spouses who are living apart differently from spouses who are living together. Under the proposed Section 118 A (3) it is provided that:

- For the purposes of an offence under subsection (1) where the spouses are living together a spouse may only refuse consent to a sexual act on any ground which may include:

  1) poor health or medical condition of the spouse refusing to perform a sexual act;

  2) evidence or reasonable fear that engaging in a sexual act is likely to cause injury or harm to the spouse refusing to perform a sexual act; or

  3) any other ground deemed to be reasonable by the court.

The effect of subsection (3) is to re-establish the right of a spouse to intimacy with an unwilling partner as long as the spouses are living together. By establishing exceptions to what would have been a general rule – that sexual intercourse (and other sexual acts) must be consensual even in a marital relationship – the proposed subsection (3) is placing a burden on the non-consenting partner to prove certain facts before that partner can be relieved of an *obligation* to satisfy the sexual needs of her/his partner.

Reading the report of the Law Reform Commission (p. xviii) it is clear that the Commission did not intend to abolish the ancient and outdated presumption of consent to sex within marriage. The Commission opens its recommendation in regard to marital rape with the words: 'The Law should continue to recognise a presumption of consent to sexual intercourse provided that:...'

I also note that the proposed law refers to non-consensual sex between married persons as 'Marital Sexual Assault' and not as rape. The use of different terminology is perhaps to communicate a message that forced sex in a marital relationship cannot be equated to and is not as horrendous as non-consensual sex outside marriage.

My conclusion is further supported by the fact that where a person is guilty of marital sexual assault (read rape by a spouse):

1. The maximum sentence is imprisonment for a period not exceeding one year (Section 118 A (2)).
2. The law provides an option of a fine.

It is provided that:

> A person convicted of marital sexual assault is liable to a fine not exceeding thirty currency points or to imprisonment for a period not exceeding one year.

Note that the court cannot order for both imprisonment and a fine.

Points to consider

Does the proposed distinction between marital rape and rape outside marriage presume that sexual intercourse achieved without the wife's consent is significantly different in character from a sexual assault by a total stranger?

Is it not possible that a rape by a spouse may be so degrading and vicious that the judicial officer should have the power to use his/her discretion to determine an appropriate sentence?

It is worth noting that the proposed Domestic Relations Bill (2003) also recognises the offence of marital rape. Under its Section 60 (1) it provides that spouses are entitled to equal rights to consortium in marriage. Under Section 60 (2) it is stated that notwithstanding subsection (1) a spouse may deny the other spouse the right to sexual intercourse on reasonable grounds which include:

- Poor health
- After childbirth
- After surgery
- During medical treatment or observation
- Reasonable fear that engaging in sexual intercourse is likely to cause physical or psychological injury or harm to the spouse denying the other spouse the right to sexual intercourse.

Furthermore, Section 61 of the proposed Bill provides that: where a person has sex with his or her spouse against the consent of the spouse, the act shall create both a criminal and civil liability, and in the case of:

a) a criminal offence, a person who commits the offence is, on conviction, liable to a fine not exceeding twenty-four currency points or to imprisonment not exceeding one year or both; and in addition, the court may direct the person to pay to the spouse, compensation not exceeding thirty currency points

Compensation in cases of sexual assaults

The Criminal Justice System can in general be criticised for ignoring victims of crime. The system focuses on the offender and thus once convicted, the offender is punished either through incarceration, or through payment of a fine to the state. It is thus said that 'victims are marginalised and their interests subsumed to society's wider interests … the state steals the victim's conflict with the offender.'[1] And Hayden and Henderson (1999) similarly noted that although victims are the proximate if secondary cause of all criminal justice proceedings, they secure little if any recognition.[2]

It is contended by many scholars that in the indigenous justice traditions of Africa, restoration of and compensation to the victim were more important than retribution. Thus in his unpublished thesis 'The Role of Chiefs in the Administration of Justice' Dlamini reported that in Africa, the central purpose of a customary law court was[3] to acknowledge that a wrong had been done and to determine what amends should be made.

In 'The Heart of Justice: Truth, Mercy, Healing, Forgiveness' (1999) Michael Lapsey[4] also contends that in the traditional societies of Africa, the first question to be asked would be: How can this damage be repaired? Goldin and Gelfand (1975:23) report that in Shona traditional society, the aim of the law is primarily to compensate the person or family wronged by the crime, rather than to inflict punishment on the criminal, although punishments are imposed as well in some cases.[5] Goldin and Gelfand further state that the award of damages to the wronged persons is of more interest to the judges than the application of punitive measures to the wrongdoer.

It cannot be doubted that a victim of a sexual assault is likely (or perhaps certain) to suffer physical as well as psychological injury. A victim often has to spend money on medical treatment. It can therefore not be doubted that there is a need to compensate victims of sexual assaults. It has been recommended by the Law Reform Commission that in addition to any penalty given to the offender, victims of rape should be entitled to compensation from the offender. In determining the extent of compensation the trial judicial officer should take into account the extent of the harm suffered, the amount of force used by the offender, medical and other expenses. The commission proposed similar treatment for a victim of defilement.

Under the proposed **Section123 (B)(1)**:

> Where a person is convicted of defilement, the court *shall*, in addition to any sentence imposed on the offender, order that the victim of the offence be paid compensation by the offender. (Emphasis mine).

It is further proposed that where the offender is incapable of paying the compensation, the victim should have access to a Victim's Compensation Fund to be set up by the State.

Note: If the proposed law is passed the judicial officer will have no discretion as to whether compensation will be given or not. As long as the offender has been convicted of defilement it is mandatory that compensation be paid.

The call for compensation in the proposed amendment is similar to what is contained in Section 348 A of Tanzania's Sexual Offences Special Provisions Act, 1998 in which it is provided that:

> When a court convicts an accused person of a sexual offence, it shall in addition to any penalty which it imposes make an order requiring the convict to pay such effective compensation as the court may determine to be commensurate to possible damages obtainable by a civil suit by the victim of the sexual offence for injuries sustained by the victim in the course of the offence being perpetrated against him or her.[6]

Recommendations on the Law of Defilement

The Commission's recommendations broaden the definition of defilement, clarify the distinction between 'minors' and 'children of tender years' and of who can be defiled.

Definition of defilement

In line with proposals for the amendment of the definition of rape, it is proposed that the prohibited act which would constitute defilement under the proposed Bill need not constitute vaginal penetration of a girl child with a male organ. It would cover other acts of a sexual nature such as anal sex and oral sex.

Another proposed change in the law on defilement is the implied message that defilement of a child under the age of 12 years is more serious than the defilement of a child who is 12 years and above. This comes out in the proposed Section 123 A (2) where it is provided *inter alia* that 'where an accused person commits defilement and the victim of the offence was at the time of the commission of the offence below twelve years of age, the person *shall* be sentenced to imprisonment for life.' (Emphasis mine). The use of the word 'shall' indicates that the maximum sentence would be mandatory.

Just as is the case under the proposed amendment to the law of rape, even in defilement both females and males can in law be victims of defilement. Thus it is provided under the proposed Section 123(1) that any person who performs a sexual act on a *child* under the age of 18 years commits an offence known as defilement.

It is also noted that defilement of children under 18 years of age would remain a strict liability offence. It would be no defence to prove that the person charged had reasonable cause to believe that the child was above the age of eighteen years (123(4)).

Another effect of the proposed amendment would be that a female adult who engages in a sexual act with a male person under the age of 18 years would be guilty of defilement. Under the current law penetrative sex of an adult female's vagina with the penis of an underage male constitutes the lesser offence of indecent assault.

The proposed amendment would also bring acts of homosexuality with an underage child into the ambit of defilement rather than the lesser offence of unnatural offences.

Consensual sexual acts between children

Under the current law, when consensual sexual intercourse takes place between a female and a male child, it is only the boy child who is penalised. Irrespective of the age difference (or lack of it) between the boy and the girl who engage in such an act, the law treats the boy as an offender and the girl is treated as a victim. The current law defines defilement as carnal knowledge of a girl child but does not differentiate between sexual intercourse involving consenting adolescents on the one hand and forced sexual intercourse with a child by another child or sexual intercourse with a child by an adult.

Where *consensual* sex takes place between a female and a male adolescent, the proposed Bill makes both partners in the above mentioned circumstances equally offenders. Thus, under the proposed Section 123 A (6) it is provided that:

> Where defilement is committed by a male child and a female child *on each other* where each such child is not below 12 years of age, *each offender* shall be dealt with as required by Part X of the Children Statute, 1996. (Emphasis mine)

Punishment for defilement of underage persons

As in the case of rape, the commission recommended that the maximum punishment for defilement be imprisonment for life. Under the proposed amendment the court would be obliged to sentence an offender to the maximum sentence under the following circumstances:

- Section 123(A)(2) where an accused person commits defilement and the victim of the offence was at the time of the commission of the offence below twelve years of age,
- or where there were aggravating factors in the commission of the offence, the person shall be sentenced to imprisonment for life.
- Section 123(A)(9): In determining whether or not aggravating factors referred to in subsection (2) exist, the court shall have regard to the circumstances referred to in subsection (3) of Section 118 of this Act.[7]

Proposed amendments to the Law on Defilement of Imbeciles and Idiots

As noted by the Uganda Law Reform Commission, the purpose of the law regarding defilement of idiots and imbeciles is *inter alia* to protect persons who are unable to give informed consent to sexual intercourse due to mental disability. Such persons are incapable of appraising the nature of the sexual act.

Noting that the phrases 'idiot' and 'imbecile' are derogatory, it was proposed that the Section should refer to 'a person with a mental disease or defect which renders the person incapable of giving consent to a sexual act.'

The Commission also noted that under the current law, women suffering from mental disability as described above are afforded lesser protection than the other category of females who are the focus of the law on defilement, i.e. girls under the age of 18 years. Whereas the current maximum penalty for defilement of underage girls is death, the maximum sentence for defilement of 'idiots' and 'imbeciles' is imprisonment for 14 years. It is thus proposed in the Bill that the penalty for defilement of persons with mental disability should be as serious as that of defilement of children. It should be the same as defilement of a child who has no capacity to give consent to sexual acts.

The Commission also noted that the current law protects females with mental disability but does not protect men with similar defects. It is thus proposed in the Bill that the law should punish any person who performs a sexual act on either female or male persons who suffer from mental illness. And in line with amendments of the provisions on rape and defilement of underage girls, a female can commit an offence of defiling a person with mental incapacity. The proposed amended section would thus read:

> A person who performs or attempts to perform a sexual act with a person whom he/she knows or believes to suffer from a mental disease or defect which renders the person incapable of giving consent to a sexual act commits an offence.

Proposed Amendments to the Law on Unnatural Offences

Bestiality (Section 145 (b))

In regard to bestiality it is proposed in the Bill that in addition to any sentence imposed on the offender, the court may order the offender to pay compensation to the owner of the animal. The amount of the compensation shall take into account:

1. the value of the animal
2. the effect of the offence on the owner
3. any other factor appearing to the court to be relevant

It should also be noted that the proposed Bill calls for a less harsh punishment in regard to bestiality than the current punishment of liability to life imprisonment. The Commission was of the view that although the community abhors bestiality, the current punishment is extremely harsh.

The Commission's study revealed that when bestiality occurs, the common reaction of the community is to make the culprit pay a fine or compensation to the owner of the animal. Culprits are rarely reported to the police. In consideration of the fact that bestiality is not perceived as a grave offence by the community but rather as an act of humiliation, it has been proposed that the penalty should be reduced to a one-year prison term.

Lesbianism as an offence

As noted in the discussion of Section 145, women who perform sexual acts on each other are not caught by the current law because they do not possess a sexual organ with which to penetrate each other. The proposed Bill would however change the situation and criminalise lesbianism. This is because what would be prohibited would be any 'sexual act against the order of nature'. It is proposed in the Bill that the section reads as follows:

> Any person who performs a sexual act with another person against the order of nature with the consent of that other person commits an offence.

The mention of the presence of consent is an attempt to make a distinction between 'homosexual rape' and consensual homosexual activity, a distinction not made under the current law.

The rule on corroboration

In its study report the Commission noted the fact that the rule on corroboration in sexual offences is unconstitutional and called for its abolition. It was also noted that Section 132 of the Evidence Act empowers courts to make convictions on the evidence of a single witness thus:

> Subject to the provision of any other law in force, no particular number of witnesses shall in any case be required for the proof of any fact.

Noting that the rule on corroboration is judge made (case) law and that judges may be reluctant to ignore precedent, the Commission recommended that a proviso specifically empowering courts to convict on the evidence of a single witness in sexual offences be appended to Section 132 of the Evidence Act.

Boys under the age of 14 years

As pointed out in our discussion of who can commit rape, the law presumes that a boy under the age of 14 years is physically impotent and can therefore not be guilty of rape as a principal in the first degree. Although the Uganda Law Reform Commission did not make any comments on this issue, I find it pertinent to discuss it. If there is in fact proof that children under 14 years can engage in penetrative sex, does it serve any purpose for the law to insist that they cannot? In several jurisdictions the common law rule has been statutorily abolished and it is useful to briefly present arguments which led to the amendment of the law in those jurisdictions. This is not however to suggest that a child who infringes the law should be treated in a manner similar to that of an adult offender.[8]

In his *Textbook of Criminal Law*, Glanville Williams observed:

> This fiction is doubly silly. First, puberty may be attained before 14, and secondly, puberty is not necessary for rape. Rape requires only penetration, not fertilisation, so that it is only an ability to have an erection, not an ability to emit semen, that is physically necessary for the crime.[9]

In South Australia, the Mitchell Committee recommended abolition of the exemption on the basis that 'a presumption which protects only boys under 14 who are capable of sexual intercourse serves no useful purpose.

In England, the Criminal Law Revision Committee in their working Paper on Sexual Offences advanced a further argument in favour of repeal thus:

> Boys under 14 are capable of sexual intercourse, however, and do in fact commit acts which would be rape if they were over 14, and the fact that they do is, we think, a matter of public concern. Cases of this kind occur in what have come to be known as 'gang bangs', that is a series of sexual assaults by a group of youths on a girl. Such cases are very serious indeed as the girl often suffers severe emotional injury as well as physical harm. The older boys will be convicted of rape and punished severely, while a boy under 14, who may have had a leading part in the rape, can only be treated as having aided and abetted. Many think it is a scandal that this should be the law. At present we can see no justification for the continued existence of this limitation of the law of rape.

It is possible that the research by the Uganda Law Reform Commission did not reveal any significant evidence that boys under 14 years of age are a source of public concern. There is a possibility that the incidence of sexual violence by boys under 14 years is negligible in Uganda. But from a child rights perspective, as well as a women's right perspective, it is still imperative that the law is re-visited.

The women's rights perspective

As earlier mentioned, some feminists have argued that the law of rape was historically intended to protect a husband's right to determine the circumstances of procreation. It was thus for this reason that originally, the emission of semen was a necessary ingredient of a conviction. Consequently a 14 year old male was exempted from the offence, since he was presumed not capable of emitting semen for conception. Today we correctly perceive rape as a violation of the victim's bodily integrity. We are keenly aware that a woman will not feel any less violated, by the knowledge that she has not conceived as a result of the sexual assault. It is thus no wonder that the slightest penetration is adequate for purposes of a conviction. It is also for this reason that I support the view that where a sexual assault on a woman takes a form other than vaginal penetration by the penis, the offender should be as seriously handled as an offender who forcibly penetrates the woman's vagina with his penis. Recognising sexual assault as inherently degrading is also the very reason why I support the recommendation that men who are victims of sexual assaults should be given the same protection as women, although men do not conceive. I find myself in total agreement with Scutt Jocelynne when she argues that:

> Loss of virginity and the fact of pregnancy arising through an attack are doubtless relevant considerations; however, these should not be primary considerations forming grounds for a male-female distinction. Pregnancy may or may not occur, and therefore cannot be a dividing line in terms of criminal liability ... notice is taken of the indignity suffered by undesirable penetration - just as presumably, should be the concern of the criminal law, equally in protecting males or females from anal penetration. It seems similarly spurious to suggest that the fact that a male cannot be rendered pregnant by means of sexual attack should lessen the interest of the criminal law in protecting him to the same extent as a female, where manner of attack and injury occurring are substantially the same.[10]

Accordingly, I would recommend the abolition of the presumption of incapacity of boys under the age of 14 years in prosecutions for offences involving penetration.

The child rights perspective

The law on defilement is presumably aimed at, among other things, safeguarding *children* and *young persons* from sexual abuse. This is in line with Article 19 of the UN Convention on the Rights of the Child and Article 27 of the African Charter on the Rights and Welfare of the Child which oblige states to take appropriate legislative measures to protect *all* children from all forms of sexual exploitation and abuse. The current provision on defilement prohibits sexual intercourse with a *girl* under the age of 18 years and is silent on the boy child. Under the current law, an adult female who has sexual intercourse with an underage boy can only be prosecuted for the less serious offence of indecent assault. The law therefore violates one of the principles basic to children's rights: the right not to be discriminated against on the basis of sex. According to Article 2(2) of the UN Convention on the Rights of the Child and Article 3 of the African Charter on the Rights and Welfare of the child, every child is entitled to rights in the convention and in the Charter, without discrimination of any kind, irrespective of the child's sex.

What are the possible reasons for the distinction between the protection availed to the girl child on the one hand and the boy child on the other? Could it be a distinction based on the fiction that a male child is physically incapable of penetrative sex and thus cannot be exposed to the more serious offence of defilement? If there is evidence that a male child has in fact been engaged in penetrative sex and the law has to protect him, it is imperative that we abolish the fiction that such child is incapable of penetrative sex. It is only then that the law can offer equal protection of female and male children from sexual abuse and exploitation.

1. Hickey C. 1999: 85, 'Alternative Dispute Resolution Within Criminal Justice' in *Restorative Justice: Contemporary Themes and Practice*, pp. 83-89. Jim Consedine and Bowen H (eds.) 1999.
2. 'Victims: The Invisible People' in *Restorative Justice: Contemparary Themes and Practice*. pp. 78-82. Jim Consedine and Bowen H. (eds.) 1999.
3. Unpublished LL.M Thesis, University of Pretoria, 1998 cited in Skelton Ann 1998 'Juvenile Justice Reform: Children's Rights and Responsibilities versus Crime Control' Paper presented at a Conference on Children's Rights in a Transitional Society. Held by the Centre for Child Law, University of Pretoria, 30th October 1998. http://www.ihr.org.za/projects/childrights/publications/jurenile.htm. Accessed September 2003.
4. In *Restorative Justice: Contemporary Themes and Practice*. pp. 45-50. Consedine J and Bowen H (eds.)
5. Goldin Bennie and Michael Gelfand (1975) *African Law and Custom in Rhodesia*. Juta and Co. Ltd Cape Town.
6. Act No.4 of 1998.
7. See discussion on the punishment for rape, page 94
8. Under the Children Statute, the law provides for the appropriate manner in which to deal with children in conflict with the law.
9. 2nd Edition, 1983, p. 237.
10.Reforming the law of Rape: The Michigan Example, 50 Austral. L.J.615

Glossary of Legal Terms

Actus reus: Guilty act. The *actus reus* is the act which, in combination with a certain menal state, constitutes a crime.

Corpus delecti: Body of the crime. Used to describe physical evidence of the corpse of a murder victim.

De minimus: The law does not care about very small matters.

In loco parentis: In the role of parents.

In rerum natura: In the nature of things.

Mens rea: The mental element of a crime.

Novus actus interveniens: A new intervening act.

Pari materia: Of the same matter, on the same subject.

Per curium: By the court. Defines a decision of an appeals court as a whole, in which no judge is identified as the specific author.

Per se: By itself, inherently

Sine qua non: Without which not. An essential condition, something that is indispensable; without which it could not be.

Stare decisis: Stand by things decided. The doctrine that, when a court has once laid down a principle of law applicable to a certain set of facts, it will adhere to that principle and apply it to future cases where the facts are substantially the same. This is a defining characteristic of the common law system.

Voire dire: Inquiry, examination

compiled with the help of *Nolo's Legal Dictionary* at http:www.nolo.com/lawcenter/dictionary/wordindex.cfm

Bibliography

Angela Davis (1983) Women, Race and Class Vintage Books, NY

Archbold Criminal Evidence and Practice 39th Edition. Sweet and Maxwell Ltd

Burke John (1976) Osborn's Concise Law Dictionary. Sweet and Maxwell, London

Card, Cross and Jones (1992). Criminal Law 12th Edition Butterworths.

Chapter 120, Laws of Uganda, Revised Edition, 2000 (Originally Chapter 106, Laws of Uganda, 1964)

Curzon L.B (1997) Criminal Law 8th Edition. M & E Pitman Publishing

Dlamini C (1998) 'The Role of Chiefs in the Administration of Justice' Unpublished LL.M Thesis, University of Pretoria. Cited in Skelton Ann (1998) 'Juvenile Justice Reform: Children's Rights and Responsibilities versus Crime Control' paper presented at a Conference on Children's Rights in Transitional Society. http://www.ihr.org.za/projects/childrights/publications/juvenile.htm Accessed September 2003.

England's Sexual Offences (Amendment) Act 1976

Freeman M. D. A (1979) 'Rape By A Husband' in New Journal Vol 129, April 1979

Geetanjali Gongoli (2004) 'The Regulation of Women's Sexuality Through Law: Civil and Criminal Laws' http://www.hsph.harvard.edu/organizations/healthnet/SAsia/repro2/regulation-throu ... Accessed on 24-06-04

Glanville Williams (1983) Text book of Criminal Law 2nd Edition

Goldin B and Gelfand M (1975) African Law and Custom in Rhodesia. Juta & Co. Ltd Cape Town

Hayden A and Henderson P (1999) 'Victims: The Invisible People' in Consedine Jim and Bowen H (eds) Restorative Justice: Contemporary Themes and Practice.

Hickey C (1999) 'Alternative Dispute Resolution Within Criminal Justice' in Jim Consedine and Bowen H. (eds)Restorative Justice: Contemporary Themes and Practice.

Ireland Law Reform Commission 1987, Consultation Paper on Rape at http://www.lawreform.i.e/publications/data/volume6/itrc-42.html. Accessed on 15.06.04

Joana Watson (2002) 'Women's Sexuality: Then and Now.' http://www.cwrl.utexas.edu/-ulrich/femhist/sexuality.shtml Accessed on 24-06-04.

Juliet Mitchell and Rose (eds) Female sexuality

MacFarlane A. Bruce (2004) 'Historical Development of the Offence of Rape' http://www.canadiancriminallaw.com/articles/toc/Hist-Dev-Rape-toc.htm Accessed on 14th June 2004

Mathew Hale (Kings Bench England, 1971)

Mcriff 'Reform of Sexual offences in Victoria: The Time to Abandon the Victorian Perspective' (1980) 4 Crim L.J 328

Lapsey Micheal (1999) 'The Heart of Justice: Truth, Mercy, Healing, Forgiveness' in Consedine J & Bowen H (eds).Restorative Justice: Contemporary Themes and Practices. Pgs 45-50.

Munir El-Kassem The UWO Gazette-Volume 96, Issue 27 at http://www.gazette.uwu.ca/2002/october/171/campus-and-culture5.htm. Accessed on 25-06-04

Murray S and Roscoe W (1998) Boy-Wives and Female Husbands: Studies of African Homosexualities. New York: St. Martin's Press.

Mushanga M (1973) 'The Nkole of Southwestern Uganda' In Molnos A (ed) Cultural Source Materials for Population Planning in East Africa: Beliefs and Practices. Nairobi East African Publishing House.

Muslim Women's League (MWL) 'An Islamic Perspective on Sexuality' http://www.zawaj.com/articles/sexuality-league.html .Accessed on 25-06-04

Onalenna Selolwane (2003) 'Talking Gender and Development' Mmegi Monitor 43, 16th August 2003.

Scutt Jocelynne (1976) 'Reforming the Law of Rape: The Michigan Example' 50 Austral. L. J 615

Smith and Hogan (1992) Criminal Law. 7th Edition Butterworths.

Southwold M (1973) 'The Baganda of Central Uganda' in Molnos A (ed). Cultural Source Materials for Population Planning in East Africa Beliefs and Practices. Nairobi: East African Publishing House.

Statute 4 of 1990

Tamale Sylvia (1992) 'Rape Law and the Violation of Women in Uganda: A Critical Perspective.' Uganda Law Society Review, 195-215.

Tamale Sylvia (2003) Feminist Africa: Issue 2, 2003

The African Charter on the Rights and Welfare of the Child. OAU Doc. CAB/LEG/24.9/49 (1990)

The Children Act, Chapter 59, Laws of Uganda (Revised Edition) 2000

The Constitution of the Republic of Uganda, Chapter 1 Laws of Uganda, (Revised Edition 2000).

The Criminal Justice and Public Order Act (1994) England

The Criminal Law Revision Committee on Sexual Offences

The Customary Marriages (Registration) Act, Chapter 248 Laws of Uganda, (Revised Edition 2000)

The Evidence Act, Chapter 6 Laws of Uganda (Revised Edition, 2000)

The Kenya Penal Code Act.

The Marriage and Divorce of Mohammedans Act, Chapter 252 Laws of Uganda, (Revised Edition 2000)

The Sexual Offences (Miscellaneous Amendments) Bill, 2000.

The Sexual Offences Act (1956) of England

The Tanzania Sexual Offences Special Provisions Act, 1998

The Trial on Indictments Act, Chapter 23 Laws of Uganda (Revised Edition) 2000

The United Nations Convention on the Rights of the Child. General Assembly Resulution 44/25

Uganda Law Reform Commission Report on Rape, Defilement and other Sexual Offences (2000)

List of Cases

Sekabazo v Uganda [1965] EA 507: **33**
Ssekitoleko v Uganda [1967] EA 53: **23**
Telesfora Alex & Another v R [1963] EA 141[1]: **29**
Tumuhairwe Vincent v Uganda Criminal Appeal No. 29/1997: **43**
Uganda v Abdalla Nassur [1982] HCB 1: **56**
Uganda v Abel Ochan [1972] (1) ULR 13
Uganda v Abel Ochan [1972] 1 ULR 13: **32, 55**
Uganda v Akua Another [1973] EA 246: **77**
Uganda v Alipakusadi Waluwayo & Another 227/1974: **73**
Uganda v Andrew Keneth Otema-Opok Crim Revision 433 of 1970: **63**
Uganda v Baturine Richard HCCSC No. 589/1996: **6, 47, 50**
Uganda v Col. Dusman Sabuni [1981] HCB 13: **56**
Uganda v Damulira [1976] HB High Court: **75**
Uganda v Ddamulia Eriabu Criminal Session Case No. 449/1995: **6**
Uganda v Dhafa Nakalyaku (1971) HCB 190: **73**
Uganda v Eddy Musasizi HCCSC No 75/1994: **6**
Uganda v Enoch Bampabura HCCSC No 135/1992: **48**
Uganda v Francis Ogema HCCr Revision 436 of 1970: **73, 77**
Uganda v Godfrey Agudi HCCSC No. 02/97: **22, 55**
Uganda v James Katumba Criminal Session Case No. 333/97 High Court: **20**
Uganda v John O. Okong HCCSC No124/1974: **23**
Uganda v Joseph Mulindwa [1975] HCB 206: **45, 48**
Uganda v Kakooza Sulaiman HCCSC 0072/1999: **33**
Uganda v Karimu Zawedde HCCSC No. 551/1996: **6, 42**
Uganda v Kezekiya Katigo Anor Crim Revision 313/1974: **78**
Uganda v Kintu Charles HCCSC 467/1995: **45**
Uganda v Kyamusungu Ivan Cr. Sess Case No. 107/1996: **4, 21**
Uganda v K. K. Shah [1996] EA 30: **29**
Uganda v Lt Col Issa Habib Galungube HCCSC No. 30/1989: **4, 31**
Uganda v Lwasa Sempijja HCCSC No. 381/1996: **44**
Uganda v Makooba HCCSC No 55/1999: **20**
Uganda v Moses Bagada HCCSC No 98/1990: **16**
Uganda v Mugisha Afranco Criminal Session Case No.69/99 High Court: **49**
Uganda v Mugoya Wilson HCCSC No 170/1993: **5, 41, 48**
Uganda v Mukasa Everisto HCCSC No. 22/1998: **45, 54**
Uganda v Mulengera (1994-5) HCB 28: **6**
Uganda v Ndosire [1988-1990] HCB 46: **56**
Uganda v Nicholas Okello [1984] HCB 22: **45**
Uganda v Nikolla and Another [1966] EA 345: **61**
Uganda v Nsubuga Daniel HCCSC No. 338/97: **46**
Uganda v Obbo Silver Toroto HCCSC No 22/1994: **43**
Uganda v Odwong Dennis and Olanya Dickson (1992-93) HCB 71: **4**
Uganda v Ojok and Another [1973] EA 489: **74, 76**
Uganda v Okello Francis HCCSC No. 52/1992: **6**
Uganda v Olungu [1972] EA 136: **74**

Index

www.ingramcontent.com/pod-product-compliance
Lightning Source LLC
Chambersburg PA
CBHW080252030426
42334CB00023BA/2784